Life in the Ranks

Life in the Ranks
The Experiences of a British Cavalryman
in Early 19th Century India

William Taylor

Life in the Ranks
The Experiences of a British Cavalryman in Early 19th Century India
by William Taylor

First published under the title
Life in the Ranks

Leonaur is an imprint of Oakpast Ltd
Copyright in this form © 2012 Oakpast Ltd

ISBN: 978-0-85706-832-3 (hardcover)
ISBN: 978-0-85706-833-0 (softcover)

http://www.leonaur.com

Publisher's Notes

The views expressed in this book are not necessarily those of the publisher.

Contents

Voyage to India	7
Ellen Harvey	13
Captain Benham and the Cornet	26
Arrival in India	32
The Chokey	37
Army Vice	43
I Hear a Confession	53
Proceed to Kirkee	64
The Rajah's Entertainments	78
Mrs B——'s Ghost	87
Attacked by Arabs	98
An Assassination	106
A Duel	115
Sergeant Morgan	123

Chapter 1

Voyage to India

Cloth of gold! Do not despise,
Though thou art matched with cloth of frieze;
Cloth of frieze! Be not too bold,
Though thou art matched with cloth of gold.

There are few lives, no matter how limited the sphere in which they have been passed, that will not furnish some passages of interest. The remark has been made by more profound thinkers than myself, and if I avail myself of it as an excuse for again obtruding on the notice of the public, I shall only be imitating the example of a host of other writers, who, with far less opportunities of observation than chance has thrown in my way, have not hesitated to draw largely on their patience.

To those who may object that a deficient education, or an humble position in life are in themselves circumstances that necessarily incapacitate one from contributing to the general stock of amusement and instruction, I have only to reply, that it is neither education, nor rank, nor wealth which in this, as in most worldly distinctions, determines one's claims to consideration; for the humbler the station in which we may be placed, and the greater the struggles we have to encounter, the more likely are we to develop qualities that would otherwise have lain dormant in pampered indolence.

Let it not be supposed, from these few prefatory observations, that I am about to inflict on my readers the important nothings of an inflated autobiography:—such is far from my intention. I desire to occupy no more prominent place in the scenes I am about to describe than the stage carpenter, or call boy, who, with no pretensions to creative power, are yet necessary to the reproduction of images which are supposed to have an affinity with nature.

The commencement of hostilities with the Burmese Empire, in 1823, rendered large drafts from our home forces necessary. I was then a young, and like most persons at that age, a foolish and inexperienced lad, entertaining a thorough contempt and dislike for everything like useful occupation; and an equally strong admiration of the pomp and circumstance of military life. When I look back to this period and recall the enthusiastic and ambitious hopes with which my young breast was filled—hopes destined never to be realized—I cannot help smiling at my own folly. And yet the retrospect is tinged with something of a melancholy feeling too, for there are few who can look upon the past without being conscious of having in some way misapplied their talents, and lost opportunities that may never again fall in their way.

During the heat of my military ardour, I one day stumbled upon the recruiting sergeant and the result is not difficult to guess. I was on my way to India with a detachment of the 4th Dragoons before I had time to reflect on the consequences of the step I had taken, but reflection being then too late I made up my mind not too add to the disagreeable realities of my position by useless repining, but to pursue the career I had chalked out for myself with a cheerful spirit and firm heart.

It is wonderful with what gay colours a little philosophy of this sort invests life. There is no state of circumstances however disagreeable that may not be divested of a portion of its unpleasantness by a disposition to view things through a contented medium. Our joys and our sorrows are mostly of our own creation and he is a fool, who knowing this, suffers his spirit to sink under the petty annoyances of life. It is Dryden I think who says, and says wisely,

> *Happy the man and happy he alone;*
> *He who can call today his own;*
> *He who secure within can say,*
> *Tomorrow do thy worst, for I have lived today.*

The voyage to India crowding as it often does, into a brief space of time, incidents enough to fill up the measure of a life, has supplied such hackneyed themes to the novel writers of the day that it was not at first my intention to dwell upon it. On reflection, however, I see no reason why the relation of actual occurrences should be omitted, because fiction has taken liberties with the subject.

As we approached Ascension Island, a suicide took place, which may be cited as a proof of the characteristic fondness of the Irish for liquor. A seaman, named O'Neil, a fine, ablebodied young fellow, having been reprimanded by the first mate for neglect of duty, turned upon him and made him some insolent answer. The circumstance was reported to the captain, and he ordered the Irishman's grog to be stopped. At eight bells, on the following day, O'Neil attended at the tub, but was refused his usual allowance. Casting a contemptuous look on the mate, he exclaimed—"Better stop my wind than my grog:" and before any of us were aware of his intention jumped overboard. The sea was running high at the time, and the ship was crowded with canvass. The captain immediately ordered the vessel to be put about, and the boats to be lowered; but every exertion to save the poor fellow proved fruitless, as he had disappeared from view before any of these steps could be taken.

I had heard and read so many marvellous stories about the rapacity of the shark, that I felt somewhat desirous of an opportunity of judging of the truth of the yarns with which the sailors entertained us—gaping landsmen. My curiosity was not long ungratified. We were within view of the coast of Madagascar, when it became necessary to take in water to fill up the empty casks. While a Portuguese seaman was employed in this duty he unfortunately overbalanced himself, and fell overboard. The sea being tolerably calm, and the man an excellent swimmer, no danger was apprehended on his account. The first mate and four of the crew prepared to descend to his assistance in the captain's gig which hung astern, but owing to the hurry of the moment the boat was carelessly lowered by the run, and the whole party immersed.

No time was of course lost in getting out another boat, but before it could be lowered the man in the fore top shouted out—"A shark, a shark! make haste, men, for your lives." A general rush was instantly made to the sides and bow of the vessel, which by this time had been put about, and the spars and rigging became also crowded with anxious spectators. A scene of fearful interest presented itself to our view, and almost every man's cheek became blanched with horror.

Within about twenty feet of the first mate, who was swimming towards the vessel, utterly unconscious of the proximity of his dangerous neighbour, was an enormous shark, whose extended jaws were already prepared to engulf his unsuspecting victim. On seeing us point at some object behind him (for hear he could not at the distance) the latter looked round, and became paralysed with terror. The monster was on the point of seizing him, when the second boat arrived opportunely to his assistance and picked him up. Cheated of his prey, the shark made for another of the struggling men, and succeeded in laying hold of a poor fellow named Andrews, who could not swim, and who was supporting himself on a hen coop, that had just been thrown overboard to him.

An imploring look, and an agonized scream, that went to the heart of every one present, told us all was over with the unfortunate man, and next minute the calm and mirror-like surface of the waters was crimsoned with his blood. The remainder of the party reached the boat in safety; but the fate of their companion, and the narrowness of their own escape, had such an effect upon them that two of the number were confined to their hammocks for nearly ten days after. When the mate, who happened to be one of them, rose from his bed, his hair had turned as white as snow!

We got becalmed for five or six weeks, after crossing the line, and consequently made but little progress. Our supply of water ran short, and our daily allowance was reduced to three pints. To such of my readers as have ever been in these latitudes, it is unnecessary to say that the privation was severely felt, and some of us endeavoured to make up the deficiency by resorting to a stratagem, the humanity of which may perhaps be questioned.

Our colonel had brought out a large mastiff with him, of a peculiarly fine breed. His affection for the animal was such as usually characterises the English sportsman; and no matter what privations we suffered on board, he took care that Neptune should not be the first to perceive them. A kennel had been constructed for him close to the boatswain's berth, and the ample trough which it contained was regularly filled with water two or three times a day by the colonel's servant. It was suggested to the carpenter, that by making a false bottom to the trough Neptune might be cheated of a portion of his daily allowance, and no one be a bit the wiser.

The carpenter set to work, and being an ingenious follow, soon improved upon the idea. Secretly removing the trough at night, he put a false bottom pierced with holes to it, and contrived so that the lower division of the vessel should communicate, by a tube, with a large tin can, which stood in the boatswain's berth below the level of the kennel. The consequence was, that when the water was poured into the trough, it found its way into the receptacle prepared for it at the other side of the partition.

Profiting largely by this simple contrivance, we kept our secret closely to ourselves, though circumstances were at times near betraying us. We could hardly contain ourselves at hearing the colonel's servant, who was a genuine Patlander, soliloquising day after day pretty much after this fashion:—

Musha, but you're the greedy crayture Nip to take sich big dhrinks, when poor divils like us are dying of drouth. May I be blessed if the baste does'nt swig as much up at a draught as would vittel the whole ship. An' he looks up at me for more too, as if he hadn't had a dhrop at all. By my sowl but he's as bad as father Rooney, who used to complain, after his twelfth tumbler, that they had given him a glass with a hole in the bottom of it.

Little did poor Paddy know how closely his simile applied.

The dog at length became almost rabid for want of water, and the colonel grew suspicious. He accused Delany, his servant, of having appropriated the animal's allowance; but the latter, than whom there was not an honester or more humane fellow in the world, stoutly denied the charge, and alleged, as an incontrovertible proof of his innocence, "that he had a mortial dislike to cowld wather;" a fact of which the colonel appeared to have a distinct recollection, from the air of conviction with which he heard his defence. Puzzled, but not satisfied, that the dog had been fairly dealt with, he resolved to see the water given to him himself, and to wait while he was drinking it.

Repairing to the kennel, followed by Paddy, carrying a large bucket of water, the colonel directed him to fill the trough, and to let the dog drink. Neptune absorbed the contents of the vessel in a shorter given space of time than ever dog or horse had done before him. The animal looked still unsatisfied—the colonel puzzled, and Paddy exulting.

"Fill it again," said the colonel, "the poor fellow is dying of thirst."

"Sorra a use in it, your honour, he's got a stomach like a sucking pump, an' there's no sich thing as satisfyin' him."

"Do what I tell you—now! that will do."

"There again, sir, you see its jist as I towld you. Its gone before you could cry Jack Kobinson."

"What can be the matter with the dog," said the colonel, quite concerned: "here Nep, my fine fellow—come here, sir."

"He won't lave the trough, your honour, you see he wants more water."

"Oh! that's nonsense, he has had sufficient already to satisfy a pack of hounds. There must be something wrong with the dog, Delany, for this insatiable thirst is not natural. You had better take him to the doctor at once, and get him examined."

"That's my own private opinion too, sir, for it isn't right for either baste or Christian to to dhrink in that way."

Neptune was accordingly taken to the doctor, and the facts having been stated to him, he shook his head incredulously at the account given of his performance by Delany. He examined the animal carefully, and declared he was free from everything like disease, but could give no explanation of the phenomenon which had been related to him. There must be a period to thirst, he said, as well as to hunger; and it was impossible that dog or human being could contain more than a certain quantity of liquid. The only advice he had to give was, that the animal should be kept under the colonel's immediate eye, and that his food and drink be given to him in his presence."

For once, and by accident, the doctor arrived at the real state of the case, and Neptune having been removed to the colonel's cabin, speedily got rid of his inordinate appetite for "dhrink."

Chapter 2

Ellen Harvey

Ah, me! that the visions of youth,
Like rainbows all melt and decay,
That the vows and the pledges of truth
Should be things that can bind but a day.

Late one night we were roused from our sleep by a sudden shock, that made the vessel reel, and led us to anticipate some terrible disaster. On rushing to the deck, I found it crowded with anxious faces, and amidst the general confusion of voices the captain's was predominant.

"What the d——l induced you to let go the wheel, you scoundrel," he exclaimed as seizing the rudder with one hand and the collar of the steersman with the other, he shook him with violence.

The poor fellow looked aghast and owing to fright or the throttling grasp of his superior, was unable to utter a word for some minutes.

"Answer me, you drunken vagabond," again thundered the captain, "or by all that's sacred I'll pitch you overboard, and give you a cooling that will soon bring you to your senses."

"I couldn't help it, sir," at length gasped out the half choked steersman, pointing at the same time to the body of a woman which lay extended upon deck, within a few feet of the binnacle.

"Hold the lantern here," cried the captain, loosening his hold of the steersman, and approaching the object indicated.

The light was instantly directed on the spot, and revealed the features of a young woman named Ellen Harvey, one of the soldier's wives, who had been permitted to accompany the detachment.

"The abandoned strumpet," exclaimed the husband who happened to be amongst the bystanders. "Was it for this she forced herself upon me. But I'll have my revenge," and clenching his fists he rushed towards the steersman.

"Stand back," roared the captain placing himself between them. "Are you all mad! Williams," he continued, turning towards the steersman, "what is the meaning of all this. The lives of everyone on board were in your keeping, and you have shown yourself unworthy of your trust."

"I own, captain, that I've been wrong in allowing my humanity like to get the better of my duty; but it all passed so quickly that the one got to windward of the other, and I somehow or other lost sight of it."

"What on earth do you mean by all this *farrago* of nonsense. I suppose you class flirting with a worthless woman, while on duty, amongst the important claims of humanity."

"You're a little out of your bearings there, captain," rejoined the steersman, "for though I own to having no great dislike to the gals, I never meddle with other men's property, and more particularly when on duty."

"Will you come to the point at once, sir," exclaimed the irritated captain, and condescend to explain why you let go the wheel."

"The fact is, captain, that about ten minutes since, as I was minding my duty, and keeping: a sharp look out ahead, I saw a petticoat stealing up from the cabin and approach the side of the vessel. Hearing a heavy sobbing like, I mistrusted the purpose of the poor crayture, and kept my eye steadily upon her, which I acknowledge was wrong, seeing that it wasn't in the line of my duty. Presently I saw the poor girl go back a bit as if to make a spring over the side, and sure enough she would have done the business if I hadn't darted forward, and catching her by her little feet, brought her to an anchor with her head downwards. When I hauled her up I found she was half dead from the blow which her head received against the side of the vessel, and I had only time to lay her alongside there when the flapping of the sails and the falling off of the vessel before the wind reminded me I had something else to think of."

"If this be true, my man, I can hardly blame you, though the consequences might have proved serious to us all. Let someone try and restore the poor woman, until we hear what account she can give of the affair."

"I think, captain, we would do well to remove her below," interposed a soldier's wife, "she appears badly hurt, and it may be some time before she recovers consciousness."

"You are right, ma'am; take her down, by all means. You, Jennings, take Williams's place at the wheel, for he doesn't seem to know what he's about, and now let us get the vessel well up to the wind."

The inanimate subject of the foregoing conversation was conveyed below, but it was long before she was restored to her senses. To most of us who knew her story, the probability of the facts related by the steersman required no confirmation from her lips. Hers was one of those dark and painful chapters of human life in which the love of woman, enduring and patient as it is, becomes tried to a degree which renders existence an intolerable burthen. Through what mental and physical sufferings must a gentle being like this have passed, who can look upon suicide and the terrible doom it entails, as a change preferable to her present state.

Men are excited to acts of desperation by false estimates of worldly honour or worldly disgrace; in nine cases out of ten, *infidels* at heart, the future has no terrors for them beyond those of physical annihilation. Not so woman—her tendencies are naturally religious; she derives a main portion of her happiness from the holy consciousness of having discharged her duties in obedience to the dictates of a creed in which she implicitly puts her trust; and her hopes of reward point as much to the future as to the present. Terrible then must be the state of mind that leads her, by one fatal act, to forfeit her chances of redemption—the promised joys of a pure and well regulated life, and the sweet hope of being reunited to those whose memories have been long treasured in her heart.

The story of Ellen Harvey is a useful and impressive lesson to those who allow their affections to overrule their reason. It may, perhaps, be deemed out of place in the diary of a rough soldier, though I do not see that there is anything in the calling to prevent us from feeling for and sympathizing with the misfortunes of others.

Daughter to a curate resident in a retired village in Worcestershire, and the youngest of a large family of children, Ellen was the pet of her indulgent parents, who bestowed on her every accomplishment that their limited means could afford. Eminently gifted both in person, and mind, she had numbers of admirers before she reached the age of eighteen, and could have been well married in her own neighbourhood had not chance otherwise ordained it. At the house of a respectable tradesman in the village, with whom her family kept up a friendly intercourse, she met a young man named Edward Harvey, whose fine, manly person and insinuating manners made an immediate impression on her young heart, a circumstance which he was not slow to perceive and take advantage of.

Harvey filled the situation of a commercial traveller to a large woollen establishment in London, and visited the village three or four times a year. On his next journey he prevailed on his friend to introduce him to the family of The clergyman, and continued regularly to visit there. It soon became apparent that he was paying his addresses to Ellen, but the clergyman, who had by this time formed a just estimate of his unprincipled and profligate character, forbid his visits when he discovered it, and told him plainly that he was not the sort of person to whom he would desire to see one of his daughters united. Harvey, in no way discouraged by this, prevailed on the infatuated girl to see him clandestinely, whenever he came round on his journeys, and to correspond with him in the interval.

Matters went on in this way for some time, when the father accidently discovered the dangerous position, in which his daughter stood. He called her into his study, and reasoned with her mildly, but firmly, on the subject.

"You must be convinced, my dear Ellen," he observed, "that in what I am about to say to you, I have no object but your own happiness at heart. I am informed that you are in the habit of privately meeting and corresponding with Mr. Harvey, and having so fully and so frequently expressed my sentiments with regard to that person, it gives me the deepest concern to find that any child of mine should encourage the addresses of a person so unworthy of her, and so displeasing to me. A connection like this, let me again emphatically repeat, can be attended with no other consequences, than future misery and disappointment, and with such opinions I can never conscientiously give my sanction to it."

Ellen's tears fell fast, and she threw herself sobbing at the feet of her father. She urged him not to make her miserable by refusing his consent to a union, which had become essential to her happiness, and stated her conviction, that the strong affection borne towards her by her lover, would give her a degree of influence over him that would soon reform his habits.

"It is useless," replied the old man, "to inflict pain on me and yourself by pressing me further on this matter. My mind is made up to what I conscientiously believe to be my duty, and I warn you that if you persist in disregarding my injunctions, you will be forever discarded from my affections."

He was about to quit the room, when the poor girl called after him in accents of despair. "Father, do not leave me in anger I will promise all that you require."

"Bless you—bless you my own good child," said the clergyman returning, and raising the now almost fainting girl in his arms. "God tempers the wind, to the shorn lamb, and these regrets will pass away."

The prediction contained in the clergyman's last words, was not however destined to be verified., The poor girl drooped, and the sorrowing parents beheld their favourite child, fast pining away. The father, firm to his notions of duty, adhered inflexibly to his resolution, and each day seemed to be hurrying her to a premature grave.

The fading girl seemed at length, however, to revive. She appeared to take more interest than usual in what was passing around her, and her spirits were occasionally wound up to a pitch of excitement, that was unnatural to her placid and melancholy temperament. Her friends wondered, but none arrived at anything like a just conclusion as to the cause of this sudden change.

One night, as the family were assembled at supper, it was remarked that the fitful mood had left her, and was succeeded by great depression of spirits. Her eyes frequently filled with tears and every effort made to divert her thoughts only served to increase her sadness.

"You had better retire to rest, my dear," said her mother at length, "you are evidently far from well, and have need of repose. Come! bid your father goodnight, and Emma will assist you to your room."

Poor Ellen rose slowly and reluctantly. Crossing over to her father she threw herself in his arms and burst into a flood of tears. The old clergyman was deeply moved, and his heart questioned him whether he was right in inflicting so much present misery on his child, to save her from that, which might, after all, be only an imaginary evil. This momentary weakness however passed away and kissing the cheek of his daughter he resigned her to her sister and requested her to lead her away.

On the reunion of the family at breakfast, on the following morning, Ellen's place was vacant. Her mother supposing her still indisposed, repaired to the little chamber that she usually occupied, but it was vacant, and the undisturbed appearance of the bed showed she had not slept there. Her drawers and boxes were lying open, and articles of dress lay scattered about in all directions, as if a hurried selection had been made of them. The truth at once flashed across the mother's mind, and anxiety and distress prevailed throughout the little household.

The following day brought back the repentant Ellen, and her husband, Harvey, to implore the forgiveness of her parents. Acting up to the spirit of the divine precepts, of which he was so worthy an expounder, the father received his erring child with parental kindness, and her husband with a delicate obliviousness of the past, which however was not needed to set the vain and confident young man at rest with himself. There are some minds so lost to all feelings of propriety and shame, that no situation, however embarrassing or awkward, can disturb their self satisfaction. Such was Harvey's, and the father could not help regretting that he could not avert the evil he had foreseen.

Harvey and his wife repaired to London after a few weeks sojourn in the village, which only served to confirm the clergyman's worst suspicions as to his character, and to increase his apprehensions for the future welfare of his child. The latter also became in some degree undeceived, though the blindness of her affection prevented her from divining all that lay beneath the surface of his as yet kind and affectionate manner.

A few short months, however, soon awoke her to a miserable consciousness of the utter worthlessness and profligacy of the man to whom she had entrusted her happiness; and yet, woman like, her love survived amidst the wreck of all her fondly cherished hopes: and she clung to the brutal being who rejected her caresses with contempt, and even violence, with an enduring devotion that excited the wonder and sympathy of all who knew her.

The periodical journeys which Harvey was obliged to make on the business of the house that employed him afforded her intervals of comparative tranquillity; but the gradual prolongation of his terms of absence soon gave rise to doubts and apprehensions, that tormented her infinitely more than the fits of ill humour and drunken caprice, to which she was subjected when he was at home. She had persuaded herself that the patient resignation with which she submitted to his will would have ultimately softened his heart, and that her better counsels would in the end prevail over the pernicious influence of the evil companions by whom he was surrounded. The conviction was however at last forced upon her that he purposely absented himself from home, and to crown her misery she learned that he spent the intervals that he passed away from her, and the money that should have gone to the support of their little household, in the company of the most abandoned of her own sex.

She dared not remonstrate, for the brutality of his temper was such that she had every reason to apprehend some act of violence on his part, which might prove fatal either to herself or the little innocent that she bore, for alas! poor Ellen was now a mother, In the mean time ruin and poverty were staring her in the face, for but little of her husband's salary went to her support; and one by one she was obliged to part with the little stock of ornaments and dress which had constituted her wardrobe at a period when it gratified her girlish vanity to deck herself out. To apply to her family was, she knew, useless, for her father had but the small and insufficient stipend of a country curate; and there were others who had stronger claims upon him than her, who had disregarded his parental counsels, and brought this miserable fate upon herself by her own wilfulness and folly.

It was not likely that dissipated habits like those of Harvey could be long kept from the observation of his employers; and although the ability which he displayed, when he did apply himself to business, induced them for awhile to overlook his irregularities, they at length became so manifestly prejudicial to their own interests that they could no longer retain him in their service.

The shock which Mrs. Harvey received from this announcement brought on a premature confinement, and it was a touching picture to see the young mother bewailing over her new born infant, the cruelty and hard heartedness of the unnatural father, who had thus left them to perish of want, at a period when all man's tenderness and care are usually evoked. The little apartment that they tenanted in itself presented an aspect of mournful privation, but too much in consonance with the actual state of facts. Cheerless and cold, without fireplace, or curtains to either bed or windows, the keen blast of a bitter March day swept at intervals through its decayed and badly hung doors, piercing its shivering tenants to the very heart, while the cries of the infant and the sobs of the suffering mother formed a melancholy accompaniment to the howlings of the wind outside.

In the midst of this scene of misery and desolation, Harvey staggered in, reeling from the effects of the potations in which he had been endeavouring to drown the feelings of selfish alarm and vexation, which the loss of his employment had momentarily awakened in his breast. Let it not be supposed that it was anything like a sentiment of remorse at having, by his wicked folly, deprived his wife and child of sustenance that he felt: on the contrary, he only regarded them as a troublesome burden, as a means of limiting his sottish enjoyments; and as such, undeserving any other consideration than that of abandoning them if he could. That he should no longer have an opportunity of gratifying his depraved appetite for pleasure, and draining the cup of vice to its very dregs, was, in fact, the sole concern the loss of his situation occasioned him.

Taking a seat beside his wife's bed, and affecting a sort of drunken levity which, brute as he was, he felt would be more appropriate in her present condition than his usual sharp tone, he thus addressed her:—

"I have good news for you, Nelly."

"Indeed! Edward—they are much wanting."

"There now! you are always whining and complaining, no matter how disposed I am to make things agreeable to you."

"Your good news! let me hear them."

"I've won the £3 I bet on the cricket match at Clapham. You never saw anything played in better style."

Mrs. Harvey groaned, but rejoined after a moment's painful reflection—

"These three pounds, where are they?"

"You know I couldn't do less than treat the party after making such a famous hit as that. We had a regular jollification of it, though I don't think it was fair of old Symmons to run the score up to four guineas against me after lodging the money in his hands."

"Great God, that you should fling away money in this way, and your wife and child perishing of hunger and cold! You are indeed heartless."

"Heartless, you jade?" said the ruffian, exasperated by this reproach, the only one that his wife had ever addressed to him—"what do you mean by that? Is it not enough that I took you from your psalm-singing beggar of a father, and ruined myself by your extravagances, but that I must debar myself from every sort of comfort and amusement, for the sake of you and your little brat?"

"Monster!" exclaimed his wife, thoroughly roused by this double insult, and raising herself by a sudden effort in her bed—"bitterly have I reason to curse you for taking me from that father; and sorely have I paid the penalty of disregarding his advice. Coward that you are, you are afraid to own to yourself that it is to your own reckless folly and misconduct you owe your ruin, and that of those who are unfortunately depending on you. But why should I waste reproaches on you; you are as incapable of feeling as reflection, and must only pursue the career your own wild passions have chalked out for you, until it is perhaps suddenly and violently checked."

For once the bully shrank before the indignant reproaches of his outraged wife, and muttering some indistinct threat, quitted the apartment.

About a week after the last scene, Harvey again made his appearance in the wretched habitation, which still owned him master, but this time it was not to insult or tyrannize over his unfortunate wife. He looked haggard and downcast, and scarcely dared to lift his eyes in her presence.

"I am come to tell you, Ellen," he said, "that I have enlisted, and shall soon be on my way to India. I know I have deeply wronged you, and the only atonement I can make, is to rid you of my presence."

Mrs. Harvey had only just risen from her bed, and had not as yet recovered her strength. It was not to be expected that this announcement, sudden as it was, would have much surprised or affected her, after the scenes through which she had lately passed, and yet the emotion with which she received it betrayed how much her feelings were still interested in the degraded and humbled being who stood before her. She burst into tears, and burying her face in her hands remained for some minutes silent. At length mastering her agitation, she beckoned to her husband to take a place beside her.

"Edward," she said, "come here. I once more recognise you. Be to me but just and kind, and whatever may be our lot—whatever may be our privations, we shall still find something to console and cheer us. The soldier's life is a hard one, but what are its hardships to our present miserable state of existence? To live as we have been living is as sinful as it is disgraceful, and Heaven only knows the agony it has caused me. Be to me again, Edward, what you once were, generous, indulgent, and forgiving; for I know I have said and done much to try your temper, and I will follow you to the world's end, smoothing your path, and supporting you under the rude trials to which you will be subjected.

"I do not expect that you will accompany me," replied Harvey, embarrassed and perhaps softened by this touching appeal. "It will be better for you to return to your family, for you are but ill fitted to brave the climate and the hardships of a military life with a young infant at your breast."

"When I accepted the obligations of a wife," said this high minded woman, "I did it in all sincerity, and I should be but ill discharging my duty, were I to desert the father of my babe when danger or sickness menaces him. Go with you I will, Edward, be the consequences what they may."

This was a result that Harvey had not anticipated, but seeing that it was useless to contest the point with her, he resolved to trust to the chance of her being unsuccessful in the drawing which was to decide the choice of the limited number of women permitted to accompany the detachment. In this, however, he was disappointed, for fortune, who seldom smiles on those who merit her favours, was in this instance propitious, and I shall not soon forget the heartfelt exclamation of thankfulness with which the young mother hugged her infant to her breast on learning that she was amongst the successful competitors.

Her lady like manners and appearance so distinguished her from the rude beings with whom she was classed, that general curiosity was excited as to the circumstances that had brought her into such a situation. This however she had too much good sense to gratify, and it was only casually that her history became known.

The alteration in her husband's manner, which had inspired her with such hopes of his permanent reformation, had passed away with the first feelings of self-abasement that had succeeded his enlistment, and he now behaved towards her with more brutality than ever. Her disappointment was of course bitter in proportion to the sanguineness of her expectations, and her gentle spirit sank under it. Almost always under the influence of his evil passions, he took every means in his power to show her that her presence was hateful to him, and yet by one of those curious inconsistencies, which often mark the characters of such men, he converted the universal attention and sympathy that his conduct towards her elicited into a ground of jealousy.

As every pretext of this sort must have an object, he selected the first mate, who had interfered on one or two occasions to prevent his using violence towards her, and in one of those paroxysms of rage, which had now become habitual with him, the ruffian became so exasperated at the indignant reply she made to one of those unjust accusations of infidelity, that he struck her in the face with his clenched fist, and stretched her bleeding and senseless on the deck.

He was instantly secured and confined; but his unfortunate wife never held up her head after. She was heard to utter no complaint or reply to the indignant comments made on his conduct by the women around her, but her countenance betrayed the internal anguish that she suffered, and it was evident that her heart was broken. She was observed to steal into the most retired parts of the vessel, and to clasp her infant in terror to her breast, as if she feared a repetition of the brutal violence of which she had been the victim, and she entreated a sergeant's wife to whom she had become much attached, to take care of her little one if anything should befall her.

These circumstances excited no suspicion of her real purpose, for it was evident that the brutal treatment she had received was gradually undermining her health, and that she felt conscious it would soon kill her. The only surprise expressed at her attempting suicide was, that she should have endeavoured to anticipate a result that was evidently so near at hand.

On being carried below, every exertion was used to restore consciousness to the unfortunate woman. It was found that she had received a severe contusion on the head, and the doctor at first entertained doubts as to whether she was not already dead. After several hours, spent in chafing her temples and feet, and in applying restoratives, she at length betrayed signs of animation, and in a few minutes more, became sensible of surrounding objects. One of the first uses which she made of her restored faculties was to inquire for her husband, and to request that he might be immediately sent for.

It was with considerable difficulty that the unfeeling fellow could be prevailed upon to enter the cabin where she lay, and that only at the command of his superiors. When he did so, it was with an air of swaggering indifference that filled every one present with inexpressible disgust.

"Edward," said the poor creature, "I have not long to live, and I cannot die in peace until you've retracted the horrible charge you made against me the other day. Whatever may have been my faults, you must at least own that I have ever been a true and faithful wife to you."

"If this is all you've brought me here for," replied the fellow unmoved, "then I shall give you no such satisfaction. You've been the cause of all my misfortunes, and it would have been well for me had you died long since."

"Hard hearted scoundrel," exclaimed one of the bystanders, unable to contain himself at this brutal answer, "are you not afraid that the

Almighty will strike you dead for thus outraging the feelings of the dying, and despising this solemn manifestation of his will."

"Leave him," said Mrs. Harvey, faintly, "he labours under some fatal delusion which has mastered his reason, and is not accountable for what he says. May God forgive and pity him."

"This comes of marrying a parson's daughter," sneeringly remarked Harvey, as he turned on his heel to quit the cabin. "They are forever psalm-singing, sermonising, and getting up scenes for the edification of the faithful. Lord bless your hearts, she has served me the same trick a hundred times before."

The effort attending this painful interview completely exhausted the little strength that the invalid had mustered to bear her through it, and she sank into a stupor from which she did not recover for some hours. A deep sigh at length gave token of returning consciousness, and she was soon able to speak to those about her.

"I have had such sweet dreams," she said to the lady of Captain C——, who had evinced great interest in her, and had been for some time watching beside her bed. "I have been again amidst the happy scenes of my childhood, and have seen my dear parents. Oh! what a smiling and tranquil picture of happiness was that home, with its calm routine of duties and pleasures, its sweet sympathies and cheerful intercourse. Do you think, madam," she continued turning towards Mrs. C——, who was deeply affected, "do you think that it is ever permitted us after death to revisit the scenes where we have been most sensible of what the world calls happiness, and to hold communion with those in whom our affections have been centred?"

"It is a sweet and consoling belief, and one for which authority might even be adduced from scriptural sources," replied Mrs. C—— unwilling to deprive the poor invalid of a hope that seemed to afford her pleasure. "It is not unnatural to suppose that though divested of its grosser matter, the soul may still cling to those pure and holy sympathies of which even our carnal nature is susceptible.

"Thank God," fervently ejaculated the poor creature, "I would gladly watch over the welfare and happiness of those whose love I cast aside for a worthless—," and the half uttered expression of a conviction which had at length forced itself upon her, was restrained by the strong sense of duty that had supported this admirable woman through her cruel sufferings.

"Will you be kind enough to tell them to bring my infant to me, dear madam," she faintly asked after a pause, during which her mind was evidently agitated by painful reflections. "The struggle will soon be over, and I must bid a last farewell to my little darling."

Her wishes were immediately complied with, and the infant having been placed in her arms, she strained it with passionate energy to her breast. What a terrible moment for the young mother!

The stillness that had hitherto reigned through the cabin was now broken by the half suppressed sobs of those who witnessed the mute agony of this touching parting. Even the doctor, habituated as he was to such scenes, turned aside to conceal his emotion.

A sudden exclamation from Mrs. C——, who had been supporting the mother's head, announced that all was over. In this last embrace of maternal love the gentle spirit of this admirable woman had passed away.

I need hardly say that her melancholy fate left a most painful impression on all on board with the exception of the heartless being to whom her misfortunes were to be attributed. Shunned and detested by his comrades he wandered amongst us like a detected felon, so distinctly was he branded by the finger of public reprobation. Of the consistent manner in which he terminated his career, I shall have occasion to speak by and by, in the order of date and locality in which it occurred.

A subscription was opened for the unfortunate offspring of this ill matched couple, and it was subsequently adopted by the kind-hearted lady who had taken such interest in its mother, on the express understanding that Harvey should never attempt to see it again, or in any way interfere with its education—a condition that he was but too glad to assent to.

Chapter 3

Captain Benham and the Cornet

And each upon his rival glared,
With foot advanced and blade half bared.

Everyone has heard of the famous triangular duel of Captain Marryatt. Now, though the affair I am about to relate cannot lay claim to as much singularity, its truth can be corroborated by stronger contemporary evidence than the witty novelist can call into court.

Amongst the ladies who accompanied the detachment, was the wife of an old Peninsular officer, named Benham, who had but lately exchanged into our regiment in the hope of obtaining in India, that promotion which his poverty denied him at home. This officer had not the good fortune to be popular with his new associates, owing to the irascibility of his temper, which had no doubt, been soured by the disappointment incident to an unassisted career like his. Of his lady's history but little was known; but her appearance and manners were of so dubious a cast, that scandal whispered she was nothing more than his mistress, and that his object in passing her off as his wife was, to save the expense of her passage out. The suspicion of such a fact was, in itself, sufficient to set the wags of the detachment on the alert, and they forthwith resolved to pay her the most devoted attention; as much, it must be confessed, from the laudable desire of annoying the waspish old officer, as of gratifying the love of admiration, which the lady so unequivocally displayed.

Though possessing some remains of beauty and a figure that might even be termed fine, Mrs. Benham was now at that period of life when ladies first begin to confess their age, and coquetry yields place to something of matronly dignity and seriousness. It was not so, however, with this determined ever-green—the fascinating smiles into which her carefully preserved features were tutored, and the meaning glance of her full dark eye showed that if the fires of passion were extinct in her breast, the love of conquest remained unabated.

For this hands, lips, and eyes were put to school,
And each instructed feature had its rule.

Her style of dress, too, though it could not be called positively vulgar, was not exactly such as was calculated to inspire a feeling of respect for the wearer. The taste displayed in the choice of colours and mode of arrangement, betrayed rather a desire to display her voluptuous beauties to advantage, than to consult the dictates of modesty or good sense, while it afforded an index to her character which might be read at a glance.

From this woman, as from a moral pestilence, the other ladies shrank with instinctive delicacy, and she consoled herself for their neglect, by attracting round her all the younger officers of the detachment. The latter were, of course, delighted at having a butt for their boisterous mirth, and ministered largely to the vanity of this superannuated Venus.

It was amusing, though at the same time pitiable to see a woman old enough to be their mother, thus enshrined as the divinity of a parcel of beardless adorers, and lavishing upon them the tender regards of amorous senility. The scene reminded one of those classical allegories in which love is represented as defying the inroads of time.

Innumerable were the tricks played upon her by her admirers; and so completely were her moral perceptions blunted by her egregious vanity and self love, that nothing was too extravagant—nothing too ridiculous for her to believe. God help the simpleton of this kind who happens to fall into the hands of military idlers. Far better for her would it be, to be thrown amongst those savage tribes who are celebrated for the ingenuity with which they torture their victims.

The inquiry will naturally suggest itself to my readers, why her husband did not interfere to protect her from the conspiracy of which she was so evidently the object. Poor man! he dared not. He himself stood in a most equivocal position, and he well knew that if he went farther than to remonstrate with her (which, with this silly woman, was totally useless) she would not hesitate to denounce him to the authorities for the imposition he had put upon them. He therefore thought it wisest to shut his eyes to the truth as long as he was able, and to take no notice of it until it was actually forced upon him. This line of conduct only confirmed the suspicions that had been previously entertained, and accelerated the result he was anxious to avoid.

One evening about dusk, as the passengers were on deck, enjoying the refreshing breeze which had succeeded the oppressive heat of the day, one of the cuddy waiters drew Captain Benham aside, and asked him what he would be disposed to give him if he placed in his hands satisfactory proofs of the infidelity of his wife. This startling, though not altogether unexpected piece of information, coming through a source from whence it would, no doubt, soon be disseminated all over the vessel, of course rendered it imperative upon him to take some notice of the matter, so he put a couple of guineas in the fellow's hand, and desired him to proceed with his story. The waiter then produced a letter, in Mrs. Benham's handwriting, directed to a young cornet, who had rendered himself conspicuous by his attentions to her, and which left no doubt on his mind as to the understanding that existed between them.

This precious epistle presented a faithful epitome of the writer's character, for after declaring her grateful sense of the many proofs of devotion that the cornet had manifested towards her, she proceeded to explain the real position in which she stood towards Captain Benham, whom she flatteringly described as a jealous old brute, and stated that she could not better testify the generous disinterestedness of her regard for him than to assure him that she would offer no very violent or unnecessary resistance, if he carried her off from her pseudo husband, on their arrival in Bombay.

The waiter explained that this letter had been found by his wife, who was stewardess of the vessel, and he supposed it had been dropped or mislaid by the writer whilst waiting an opportunity of privately delivering it to the cornet.

Captain Benham desired the man to preserve strict secrecy as to the affair, and to recommend his wife to do the same, and then walking up to the cornet, who was standing on the quarterdeck in conversation with some of his brother officers, he begged the favour of a few minutes' private conversation with him in the cuddy. The young man instantly complied with his request, and followed him below.

Having shut and bolted the door of the cabin, which luckily for his purpose happened to be empty, the captain turned round and confronted the young officer with as much coolness as he could command.

"So you are carrying on a clandestine correspondence with my wife, Sir," he exclaimed in a voice trembling with suppressed rage.

"I, Captain Benham, I protest I never even dreamt of such a thing."

"And you are only awaiting our arrival in India to carry her off."

"You must be mad," said the young man staring at him in an attitude of the most ludicrous surprise, "nothing was ever further from my intentions."

"I see you do not scruple to add falsehood to the treachery and rascality of your conduct, Sir; but your meanness will avail you nothing. I hold proofs of what I assert in my hand."

"Then, before we go farther, perhaps you will allow me to see them."

"No," said Captain Benham, who had his own reasons for withholding the letter, "I will afford you no further ground for equivocation or evasion. 'Tis enough to say that I am fully satisfied of the truth of these charges, of which indeed no stronger evidence need be adduced than your attentions towards Mrs. Benham since her arrival on board."

The cornet felt there was some justice in the latter part of this remark, so made no further attempt at expostulation.

"I see there is no use in reasoning with you. Captain Benham, though I cannot but feel you are doing me a gross injustice. As you are determined to hear no explanation from me, you can have but one motive in bringing me here; and, indeed, the strong language you have just used renders such a result inevitable. The only thing now to be considered is, how are we to effect it in a crowded vessel like this?"

"Oh! there is no difficulty about that. Secure the services of a friend, and meet me on deck at midnight. There is not much chance of our being disturbed at that hour, if we keep the matter to ourselves. By the bye, you have pistols I believe?"

"I have."

"Then get your second to load them, and bring them with you. We must lose as little time as possible in making preparations on deck, as it would only have the effect of attracting attention to our movements. I have no pistols with me, so shall be satisfied with the choice of yours. It is agreed we meet at twelve?"

"At twelve to the minute."

"Good morning 'till then," and the old captain touched his hat, with formal politeness, to his opponent, who returned the salutation with the same stiff courtesy.

The night set in unusually dark, and it was difficult to discern any object distinctly at more than a few paces distant. Nearly the whole of the passengers had retired to rest, and of the crew no one but the steersman and the lookout were visible on deck when the duellists stole up to their appointment.

The ground was soon measured, and the principals placed in a line drawn diagonally from side to side, so as to leave a sufficient distance between them, and at the same time keep the man at the helm out of pistol range.

Not a sound was to be heard, except the moaning noise made by the main mast as it strained under the weight of its heavy sail.

"Are you ready," cried the seconds appointed to give the word.

"Ready," replied both the principals.

"Fire."

A terrific explosion followed, which shook the vessel to its very centre. From the windows of the fore and after cabins, the hatchways and various other parts of the vessel sharp reports and strong flashes of light succeeded each other in rapid succession, and even the two signal guns that stood on the quarter deck simultaneously bellowed forth their contents. To add to the astounding effect of this unexpected *coup de theatre*, piercing screams and loud peals of laughter might be heard on all sides, but from whom they proceeded it was impossible to say, as no one was visible except the man at the helm, who calmly pursued his occupation without appearing in the least disturbed by this "crash of elements."

Nothing could exceed the dismay and astonishment of the duellists at this sudden and unlocked for interruption to their proceedings. They stood staring at each other for some minutes in mute surprise, with mouths open and arms extended, like men who had succumbed to the paralysing influence of a supernatural visitation.

The old captain was the first to recover himself, and turning on the seconds he angrily said,

"It is to you we owe this piece of buffoonery, gentlemen, but by heaven you shall both answer for it on the spot."

"Excuse me, Benham," said the colonel, who had just ascended from the cabin, followed by a group of merry faces. "The ladies have had enough of gunpowder, and must not be again frightened in this way. From what I have just ascertained, from the real authors of the joke, I can fully exonerate these gentlemen from the charge you have brought against them. Nevertheless, I shall feel it my duty to place you all under arrest, unless you give me your parole that we shall not have a repetition of this discreditable scene."

"I shall give you no such thing, sir," furiously replied the captain. "I will not be made the butt and the plaything of a parcel of silly boys."

"Then, if such be your determination, sir," said the colonel sternly. "I shall instantly place you under arrest, and bring you to a court martial as soon as we arrive in India. Recollect that you are the party most to blame in this affair. I will not allude more specifically to the error you have committed, but a moment's reflection will suffice to convince you that, the less that is said or known about it the better."

"You are right, Colonel W——," said the old officer, restored to himself by this hint, "I will do all that you require."

Thus ended this most extraordinary scene. Although it may well be supposed that the captain did not feel extremely comfortable under the sly innuendoes with which he was constantly assailed on the one side, and the taunts and reproaches which greeted him on the other; he bore them all with more philosophical resignation than might be expected from his temperament, and on our arrival in India rid himself both of one and the other, by sending his mistress adrift, and exchanging into the infantry.

CHAPTER 4

Arrival in India

Des singes empaillés, des serpens en bouteilles,
On me tarirait pas sur toutes ces merveilles.

We arrived within sight of the lighthouse of Bombay, about the middle of November, and those who have been pent up for months in a small and crowded vessel, can well understand the feelings of joy with which we hailed the prospect of our approaching deliverance.

Some few there were, however, who looked upon our release with very different feelings. Friendships and attachments had been formed and cemented during the progress of the passage that were destined to be interrupted or broken up by this event; and those who had abandoned themselves to the delightful intercourse which so soon springs up between kindred feelings and tastes, could not help manifesting their regret at its speedy termination. There were others, too, who felt a sad consciousness that they were approaching the European's grave, and painful memories crowded upon, and depressed them; their pale and dejected countenances reflecting but too faithfully the character of their thoughts, and forming a sad contrast with the joyous faces around them.

There is little in the appearance of Bombay to impress the stranger at first sight, though a careful examination of its position shows that it possesses advantages that few other ports can boast of. The town is situated on the S.E. extremity of a small island, separated from the main land by an arm of the sea, and with the contiguous islands of Colabah, Salsette, Butcher's Island, and Caranjah, it forms one of the safest and most commodious harbours in the world. The lighthouse stands on the southern extremity of Colabah island, and it may be seen in clear weather at the distance of seven leagues. The point which it occupies is surrounded on all sides by an extensive reef of rocks which is divided into prongs, of which the most dangerous stretches S.W. about three miles from the lighthouse.

The varied and picturesque scenery of the coast, so different in its character from any thing we had before seen, and the singular costumes of the natives, who came swarming round the vessel in their boats offering various wares for sale, as well as the novel nature of the commodities themselves, had all a new interest for us, and we felt ourselves as it were suddenly transported into another and more primitive world, where civilization had its task to commence, and where nature might be seen rioting unfettered by the hand of art.

The natives are proverbial for their expertness in diving, and we witnessed several amusing feats of this sort. Some bottles were flung into the sea, and the chattering occupants of the nearest boats immediately plunged down after them, and after a submarine contest, the lengthened duration of which astonished us Europeans, they were brought to the surface in triumph.

After remaining a few days in Bombay, we embarked in *pattemars*, and were conveyed along the coast to a town called Cambay, situated at the mouth of the gulf of that name, at a distance of about seventy miles from the Presidency. The country surrounding it is of a wild and uninteresting character, and the only production for which it is remarkable is the beautiful agate with which its sandy soil abounds. Although this mineral is found in Ceylon and some other parts of India, it is to be met with in largest quantity and greatest perfection in this district. The principal mines of agate are situated in the principality of Rajhpepla, within fourteen miles of the City of Broach.

The day after we arrived at Cambay, we lost four men belonging to the detachment, the intense heat producing an immediate effect on such of the Europeans as were at all debilitated in constitution. Horses having been sent down for our conveyance, we started on the following day for Kaira, which is about forty miles distance from Cambay.

Our road lay through a thick jungle, infested by wild beasts, and abounding in game of every sort. The monkey tribe attain a larger growth here, than in almost any other part of India, some of them measuring from four to five feet in height, and possessing a degree of agility and strength that renders them formidable even to the human species.

The sick, amongst whom I had the ill luck to find myself, were conveyed in a *hackery* or covered cart, drawn by bullocks, and attended by a native driver; but owing to the indifference of the road we could not keep up with the remainder of the detachment. Between the tremendous jolting of the vehicle during the day, and the incessant howling of the jackals during the night, it may well be imagined our situation was far from comfortable. So intolerable became the latter nuisance, that a Scotchman named Wallace, who had the charge of the party, and who was the only one of us whose strength was not completely prostrated, lost temper, and arming himself with a stout cudgel, commenced beating the jungle, in order to scare the jackals away. He had hardly quitted the cart, when a sudden exclamation from one of the invalids, who lay nearest the curtains which protected the entrance of the vehicle, called our attention towards him.

"Ugh!" exclaimed the poor fellow shuddering and shrinking back as a huge paw was thrust through the curtains and planted on his breast. Next moment he absolutely screamed with fright, as a grinning face presented itself at the opening and took a leisurely view of the interior.

The moon was not yet up, and the obscurity which prevailed added additional terrors to this unexpected apparition. Not a man of us was able to move hand or foot, so completely had fever prostrated us.

"'Tis the devil!" cried one.

"'Tis a whole troop of devils," exclaimed another, as about a dozen equally hideous faces came peering curiously over the shoulder of our first visitant.

"The monkeys are upon us! fling that bottle at them, Tom."

"Monkeys be d———d!" said the party addressed, "who ever saw monkeys like that."

In hopped the leader of the party on the chest of the last speaker and stifled his utterance. He was instantly followed by his companions, and we had nothing for it but to lie patiently and allow them to have their way.

The provisions were suspended from the ribs of the awning which covered the *hackery*. The wine bottles and physic vials hung at the sides.

"Watch that hugly looking thief how he munches the biscuits."

"They'll find out the drink presently: I hear Master Jacko jingling the bottles in the corner there."

"I'd give a month's grog if they'd only take a taste of the black draught."

A hissing and spluttering sound, followed by the cracking of glass against the side of the cart, announced the consummation so devoutly to be wished for. A loud burst of laughter resounded from one end of the vehicle to the other. The monkeys stopped short in their operations, and cocking their ears, appeared to deliberate as to the prudence of beating a retreat. Seeing the effect our involuntary merriment had produced, we hastened their decision by another simultaneous shout, which sent them all scampering into the road, with the exception of a couple of old stagers who remained grinning and chattering fiercely on the steps of the vehicle.

At this juncture Wallace returned, and we heard him laying his cudgel about him with a hearty good will. Our two friends at the entrance saved themselves by jumping on the roof of the cart, from whence they confronted him with spiteful looks.

I should have mentioned that the native driver remained an inactive spectator of this curious scene, the monkey being held sacred by his caste, and any attempt to molest it considered a serious offence against the laws of his religion.

The Scotchman, unaware of this fact, began swearing at him for his cowardice, when he was saluted by a volley of stones and branches which came showering on him from all sides of the jungle. Whilst standing completely bewildered by this general assault, one of the malicious animals, who was perched upon the roof, made a sudden spring, and calculating his distance with admirable nicety, dropped with his full weight on the Scotchman's head, and laid him sprawling on the earth.

The wood resounded with a chattering *io paean* of triumph at this signal overthrow; but Wallace recovered himself in an instant, and made an effort to grapple his hairy assailant. The latter was, however, too nimble for him, and succeeded in making his escape to a neighbouring tree, from whence he joined in the general chorus of this legion of devils. Wallace, exasperated at the rough treatment he had met with, loaded his gun, and soon brought down Master Jacko from his triumphant perch. His companions terrified at his fate, fled in all directions, and the Scotchman had the satisfaction of finding himself in victorious possession of the field.

On the following day we arrived at Kaira, which was at that time the military station of Guzzerat, and the head quarters of the regiment to which I belonged. Its site is extremely picturesque, and a neat church and commodious barracks give it quite the appearance of an English town. It is surrounded by a lofty stone wall, with semicircular bastions in good repair; and the streets included within its circumference are clean and well kept, though narrow. The houses are solid and lofty structures, with sloping, tiled roofs, and the gables are in general profusely ornamented with wood carvings, representing obscene subjects from the Hindoo mythology.

The situation of Kaira is about the worst that could have been pitched upon for a military station, it being annually visited by fever, dysentery, and cholera *morbus*.

There is a temple here devoted to the worship of a peculiar caste of Hindoos, called the Jains, but their priests would not allow us to enter it. This sect holds the peacock in especial veneration, and there was formerly a wooden idol, with diamond eyes representing the bird in the temple, but the cupidity of the priests has, I suppose, found more useful employment for the eyes of the god elsewhere, as they no longer dazzle the reverential gaze of its worshippers.

Most of the inhabitants of the district being of this caste, peacocks are to be found in great abundance in almost all the farm yards in the adjoining villages. Now, this bird, beside being pretty to look at, is by no means bad eating, though it cannot be compared to a good English turkey. My comrades were in the habit of making excursions in quest of it, as soon as night set in, but as I have already mentioned, it was held sacred by the natives, and as any invasion of their property or religious prejudices was likely to be severely punished by the authorities as well as revenged by the owners, it became necessary to observe the utmost secrecy and caution on these expeditions.

Being young, adventurous, and new to the country, strong inducements were held out to me to join one of these marauding parties; but fortunately for myself I had not as yet been sufficiently inured to Indian life to have lost the power of distinguishing between justice and oppression. I could not look upon the natives in the same light as my comrades, who regarded them as beings of an inferior stamp, whom it was right to trample upon and rob whenever the opportunity presented itself. It was well for me that I had retained sufficient principle to prevent me falling into a snare that might have cost me my life, or left me subject for sorrowful reflection for the remainder of my days.

The details of this nocturnal adventure, as related to me by one of the parties concerned, are curious enough as showing how the love of excitement will induce men recklessly to hazard their own lives or endanger those of others.

Chapter 5

The Chokey

There are human natures so allied
Unto the savage love of enterprise,
That they will seek for peril as a pleasure.

It was a bright moonlight night, and all nature seemed buried in profound repose, as four men in the uniform of soldiers might be seen wending their way through the rich expanse of corn fields in which the little village of Lucknee lay embosomed. It was evident from the straggling and unsteady gait of the party, as well as the angry tone in which they debated some disputed point, that they had been freely indulging in liquor; and although one of them, who appeared to have retained some degree of self-command, frequently impressed upon his companions the necessity of observing a strict silence as they approached the village, his advice, as might be expected only had the effect of rendering them still more boisterous,

"You will get us into a scrape, Jamieson, if you continue to make such a confounded noise," said this person to the most obstreperous of the party, "You really must be silent."

"You be d—— d," politely replied the party addressed, "don't think you're going to do the captain over me," and at the same time he executed a most difficult movement, by letting his head and shoulders sway gracefully on one side while his legs made a pirouette on the other, until the equilibrium of the rebellious members was restored by a desperate effort from the centre.

"It will never do to make the attempt in the condition we're in at present," observed the first speaker to another of the party. "There is Jamieson completely cut, and Kerr is little better."

"Drunk's the word," exclaimed Jamieson, "don't be ashamed of it, Bob. Drunk as a lord, but what does that signify. I'm ready for anything, old boy!" and he made another evolution such as I have described, but with less success than before, as he lost his balance and came heavily to the ground.

His companions made repeated efforts to set him on his feet again, but no purpose, as he had lost all power of maintaining himself when there.

"It's no use," hiccupped Kerr, who had nearly equal difficulty in preventing himself from falling, "he has no bones in his legs, the beggar."

"What's to be done, Marshall?" said Roberts in despair to his other companion. "It would be madness to think of persevering in our plan tonight. If the Jains hear us they will be upon us in a moment, and these poor fellows are too far gone either to fight or run for it."

"The best thing we can do is to get over into that *tope* yonder, and try what an hour or two of sleep will do for us. The night is early yet."

"We've nothing else for it, I fear; so do you take Jamieson by one arm, and I will hold him by the other. Kerr, we're going to take a snooze amongst the trees there, so come along."

"No, I'll take a stretch here," replied the latter, laying himself comfortably down.

"This will never do," said Roberts. "You will certainly be discovered here, and, probably, have your throat cut."

"What does it matter if I know nothing about it. It's as short a way as any of kicking the bucket."

"Then kick it and be d———d," said Roberts, losing all patience, and leaving him to his fate.

Having carried Jamieson over to the *tope*, which afforded, as they thought, abundant means of concealment, they lay down to rest, and in a few minutes the whole party was snoring soundly.

"I say, Roberts, leave off your tricks," exclaimed Jamieson, suddenly awaking, some hours after, on receiving a violent chuck which had the effect of thoroughly rousing him. On looking up, he found himself surrounded by half a dozen grinning natives, who were in the act of pinioning his arms, while a number of others were engaged in securing his companions.

"You black thieves," shouted Jamieson, in the impotency of his rage, "just loosen me for about ten minutes, and I'll show every mother's son of you the difference between an honest Scotchman and a parcel of sneaking Gruddars[1]."

The natives grinned and made some in which the word *chowdrie* was frequently employed.

"They want us to go before the native magistrate," said Roberts, "and as they have possessed themselves of our arms, and skewered us like chickens, we had better yield with a good grace."

"May I be d——d if I do," said the obstinate Scotchman. "I'll not be driven like a sheep before a set of treacherous beggars like these, that I could pummel by scores if my arms were free."

"What a mulish animal you are, Jamieson," said Roberts, "you'll be forced to do it whether you like it or not, so take a friend's advice, and submit quietly to what you can't help."

"*Chowdrie, chowdrie,*" again cried the natives making significant signs to us that they would use force if we did not at once proceed where they indicated.

"Let's be off," said Roberts to the other two men, "or we shan't get out of this affair with whole bones."

He accordingly intimated his willingness to move on, but Jamieson refused to stir from the sitting posture which he had occupied during this dialogue.

The natives looked puzzled, and exchanged a few words with each other. Four athletic looking fellows precipitated themselves upon him, and seizing him by the arms and legs bore him kicking and swearing to the village.

In this manner the party made their appearance in presence of the *chowdrie*. The magistrate was seated cross-legged on a mat, but the air of official gravity which he had assumed, gave way at once before the grotesque appearance which the Scotchman cut. His clothes were hanging in tatters about him from the efforts he had made to free himself; his pimpled face was swollen to more than its usually large dimensions, and was now of a bright purple colour.

The *chowdrie* repressed the smile which had lit up his really good natured features, and in tolerably good English inquired their motive in coming to his village. Frequent robberies he said, had of late been committed in Lucknee by the soldiery, and some of the natives had been dangerously wounded in endeavouring to defend their property. The constant repetition of such offences had obliged him to set people on the watch, and the suspicious circumstances under which the prisoners were found in his neighbourhood, rendered it his duty to

---

1. Jack-asses.

make some inquiry into the purpose of their visit.

Roberts, who acted as the spokesman of the party, replied that they had been out shooting, and had no intentions of a dishonest nature. He hoped that the magistrate would order their arms to be restored to them, and allow them to return quietly to their barracks.

"And I say old cock," added Jamieson, who had not entirely recovered from the effects of the previous night's potations. "If you'll just tell your black bums to loosen these confounded girths, it'll do your heart good to see the milling I'll give them."

"The explanation you have given me," said the *chowdrie*, not appearing to notice this ill-timed sally, "is far from satisfactory, and it will be my duty to keep you in confinement until I have time to communicate with the military authorities. Remove these men to the *Chokey*," he added to the guard, "and watch them carefully, so as to prevent them making their escape."

Roberts remonstrated earnestly against this decision, which happened to be the thing of all others that he most desired to avoid, knowing well that severe corporal punishment would be the consequence; but the *chowdrie* remained firm, and they were marched to the *Chokey* or guard house, Jamieson using the only members he had free in bestowing occasional kicks on the guards.

The building dignified with this title was a miserable thatched hut, having a partition, which separated the male and female prisoners, and doors of tolerable strength. It was thatched with layers of grass.

"What a pretty pickle we have got ourselves into," exclaimed Roberts despondingly, as he heard the doors locked upon them. "What is to be done now? If the *chowdrie* sends to the barracks we shall be brought back by a strong guard, and tried by court martial for being absent without leave."

"Anything sooner than that, boys, we'll force the crib," said Marshall, approaching the doors and examining them.

"And get shot for our pains," replied Roberts. "In the first place, the doors are too thick, and in the next there is a guard stationed outside."

"I've got out of a worse scrape than this, by the aid of a little ingenuity. What you say is true enough, but there are other means of escaping without forcing the doors."

"Let us hear your plan then."

"As soon as the evening sets in, and that we have no reason to apprehend any further visits we will commence working our cords against the angles of the door posts, and will soon free ourselves from them. I will then cut a hole through the roof, without making much noise, and if there be men stationed below we can drop upon them and take to our heels in the confusion."

"Nothing can be better, but instead of waiting until evening to work through the cords, do you commence immediately, and get your hands free as soon as possible. Should any one come in, you can keep them behind your back as if still tied, and we will divert attention from you. When the evening arrives you can liberate us, and we will not be long in working through the roof."

The plan having been agreed upon, no time was lost in putting the first part of it into execution. The ligatures were soon sawn through by the friction of the door-posts, and Marshall was at liberty.

Several visits of inspection were paid in the course of the day by the *chokiedar* or jailor; but they became less frequent towards the fall of the evening, and as soon as the last meal had been served, the prisoners proceeded to put their project into execution.

Having liberated his companions with a large knife, which he had in his pocket, and mounted the partition, Marshall began cutting away the thatch with the same instrument, and in a short time had made a hole large enough to put his head through. He peeped cautiously out, and saw three men seated immediately under him, quietly smoking their *chillums*. Their bows and matchlocks stood against the walls of the hut.

"It's just as I expected," said Marshall drawing in his head. "Let us cut away the inner part of the thatch part here, and when I give the word, push the remainder into the road, jumping immediately after it, so as to a rail ourselves of the confusion it will occasion.

This having been done, at a word from Marshall, the frail roof tumbled in large masses into the street, burying those below in a heap of rubbish, and at the same moment the four prisoners precipitated themselves upon the confused and astonished guard, who believed the hut had fallen upon them.

To seize their swords and matchlocks was the work of an instant. Stunned and bewildered, they offered no resistance, and the remainder of the guard who came up to their assistance were soon overpowered.

"To the house of the *chowdrie*," shouted Roberts, "our arms are there, and we must not return without them."

The village by this time was in an uproar, and men, women,

and children were recklessly knocked down or overturned in their progress.

Gaining the house of the magistrate, they forced the doors and soon reached the apartments where their arms were kept. The old magistrate had escaped at the first alarm.

"Now lads," said Roberts, "the worst is to come. I hear the natives assembling outside, and we shall have to fight our way through them. See that your pieces are loaded, but only use them at the last extremity, for I fear we shall have enough to answer for as it is. Let us make a rush together, but do not separate, or we shall all be massacred."

On emerging into the narrow passage or lane in front of the house, they found an immense mob armed with weapons of every sort. They were received with a volley of stones and arrows; but, striking about them with the butt end of their pieces, they had nearly fought their way through, when Jamieson received an arrow in the breast which stretched him lifeless on the earth.

Exasperated at the fate of their companion, they presented their guns at the crowd and swore they would shoot the first man that attempted to stop them. Nothing intimidates a mob so much as fire arms, and the threat had the desired effect. They succeeded in gaining the open country, and reached their barracks in safety; but were immediately placed under arrest, and sentenced to three hundred lashes by a court-martial summoned to investigate the offence.

Chapter 6

Army Vice

And every brother rake will smile to see
That miracle a moralist in me.

That habits inimical to the health and morals of the British soldier prevail to a more alarming extent in India than in any other of our military stations, whether at home or abroad, is a fact that will not admit of dispute, although there may be some difference of opinion as to the causes to which it is to be attributed. Notwithstanding all that has been said and written on the subject, it strikes me that an important feature of the inquiry has been altogether lost sight of, namely, as to how far the present canteen regulations may assist in checking or aggravating the evil.

To most persons unacquainted with the country, the assertion will no doubt appear strange, that the restrictions imposed by the authorities on the quantity of liquor allowed to each individual, and the time at which it is to be served out, are calculated to produce an effect directly contrary to that which is intended. Such is, however, my firm belief, and if my readers will bestow a few minutes patient attention on the subject they will perhaps concur with me in opinion.

Equal, if not superior, in physical organization to the troops of almost every other country, it has often been demanded why the soldiery of Great Britain stand so much lower in the social scale. The answer is a simple one—because the whole scope and tendency of military legislation is calculated to degrade the soldier in his own estimation, and to leave his moral feelings no room for play. He is regarded as a mere animal endowed only with brute instincts, and the consciousness of this humiliating fact lowers many a highly gifted and sensitive mind to the common level. Once a man's sense of moral responsibility is destroyed, it cannot be expected that he will become either a good soldier or a useful citizen.

The motives that incite other men to exertion, and the feeling of self respect which prevents them from yielding to temptation, are wanting in his case; for it seems the policy of the military code not to encourage anything which might develop his better instincts or elevate his mental faculties. Dealing with the material of which the mass is composed as brute matter, the agency by which it is shaped, and fashioned into the automaton form, dignified with the name of soldier, is of corresponding harshness and severity. Penal regulations and restrictions greet the unfortunate tyro at every side, and the few indulgences that his hard lot admits of are watched and curtailed at the pleasure of his superiors. Is it to be wondered at, therefore, that he should feel a sort of savage gratification at breaking through restraints which those in authority do not impose on their own conduct, and which savour of unnecessary despotism. Hatred of oppression seems a principle implanted in our nature, and to this impulse, rather than to any real passion for the vice prohibited, may be traced much of the evil complained of.

But there is another objection to the present regulations, which appears to me to possess even greater force. To any person of ordinary reflection it would seem impolitic on the face of it, to drive the soldier from his barracks in quest of an indulgence which he ought to find there. In the first place, the *wallop* or spirit of the country is one of the vilest and most unhealthy compounds that was ever distilled, and the constant use of it must ruin the constitution. In the second, the moment he leaves the barracks, he is beset on every side by temptation, inveigled into the lowest and most abandoned society, drawn into drunken broils which often terminate fatally, and then disgraced and punished. If the love of drink be so confirmed as not to be easily corrected or eradicated, in what is the condition of the unfortunate man, or the discipline of the regiment benefitted by his being driven to indulge the propensity abroad.

Wives are generally heard to say that if their husbands must get drunk, they would be far more satisfied if they would indulge at home, for then they would be able to keep them out of mischief. If our military rulers would only condescend to borrow a hint from female tactics, they would find their task a much easier one, and those over whom they are placed would reap incalculable benefits from the change. In civil legislation prevention is held to be better than punishment, and it has the additional recommendation of being more merciful towards those likely to infringe its rules. I can see no reason why this principle, sound and humane as it is, should not be advantageously applied to military government, and the removal of the foolish restrictions to which I have alluded would have a double influence in furthering such a result, first by leaving it entirely to the good sense and manly feeling of the soldier himself to use or abuse the indulgence as he pleased, and secondly, by retaining him under the immediate observation of his superiors who would thus be in a position to check his excesses, or at all events to prevent him from doing mischief to himself or others, by sending him to the guardroom to sleep off the effect of his potations.

If there be any truth in the opinions I have advanced, my readers will arrive with me at the conclusion that while a strict surveillance should be kept over the soldier in reference to the correct performance of his military duties, it is unwise to lay unjust restrictions on his moral conduct—a conduct for which he is alone amenable. In every other relation of life we find it is not only more agreeable but easier to persuade than to compel to the performance of that which is right; and I cannot see why the soldier should be exempt from the common influence. Satisfy him that something relating to the honour of his position as a member of the community—something having a tendency to promote his own individual happiness and respectability has been left to himself to perform—in a word, elevate his sense of moral dignity by showing a confidence in his power of discriminating between right and wrong, and it will be found that although in some, perhaps in many instances, the liberty may be abused, yet on the whole it will work out a remedy much more efficacious and permanent in its effects than martinet regulations, which are based neither on principles of policy nor humanity.

It has been urged as an excuse for indulgence in this degrading vice that the excessive heat of the climate renders a certain degree of stimulus necessary to the constitution of Europeans. I cannot admit the validity of such a plea, for my own experience and observation of others, lead me to form a directly contrary opinion. I have frequently heard a similar explanation given in England to foreigners who have made remarks on the general tendency of the people to indulge in the use of ardent spirits. What analogy is there between the two climates which admits of an equal application of the rule? The humidity of our English atmosphere may, to some extent, justify the use of spirits; but, unfortunately for the arguments of the Indian consumer, the temperature of the districts in which drunkenness most prevails, affords no such excuse. The inconsistency can only be reconciled by the same process of reasoning by which the natives of the Green Isle have arrived at the conclusion, that a great coat keeps out the heat as well as the cold.

In every other climate but that of India, it is considered wise to adapt one's habits to those of the natives, as they must necessarily be based on principles suited to the temperature or other circumstances of the country. Now the natives themselves, with the exception of the veriest dregs—the lowest caste of society, or more strictly speaking, those who belong to no caste at all, are reared up to habits of the most rigid temperance, and are religiously taught to abhor all transgressions of its rules. It is quite true that amongst the Mussulmen, instances are not wanting in which infractions of the commandment of the prophet sometimes occur, but such cases are comparatively rare, and being usually practised in secret, the danger of a mischievous example is avoided. But the most convincing proof of there being nothing like a physical necessity for the constant use of spirits is the fact, that the Europeans who acclimate themselves by accommodating themselves to native habits, are those whose constitutions longest resist the enervating influence of a tropical sun and the sudden attacks of epidemics to which the excessive heat renders them liable.

It may be thought that I am attaching too much importance to this subject, but to anyone who is at all familiar with the extent of the prejudices I have been endeavouring to combat, and their fatal influence on almost every class of our countrymen in India, the stress which I lay upon it will not appear exaggerated. Deeply, most deeply have I deplored the daily occurrence of scenes occasioned by this mad infatuation, which must have presented the character of the Christian and the European under the most disgusting and revolting aspect to the pure and simple minded Hindoos. What must they think of the religion to whose tenets we would convert them, which cannot restrain its votaries from degrading themselves below the level of the brutes of the creation. The term, *mud walla*, the Hindoo expression for a drunkard, is strikingly appropriate, and conveys some notion of the contempt with which they regard the character.

It is worthy of remark that upon the arrival of a fresh batch of recruits from Europe, there is not, perhaps, one out of ten who does not evince a strong dislike to the spirit which is served out to him on his arrival, and who does not make wry faces while endeavouring to force it down. In most instances it is given away, and as eagerly caught at by some old and steady-going tippler. A few weeks, and even days suffice, however, to produce an entire revolution in opinion, caused in the first instance by the raillery of others, and then by an acquired taste. In a short period the youth who would have shrunk from the idea of a debauch, feels himself irresistibly led to adopt habits of his more tried Indian associates, and in process of time becomes himself initiated and the initiator of others.

Under the old regulations the first thing served out to the troops, whether in quarters or the field, was the ration dram, which was about equal in measure to what is termed in this country a gill. This taken upon an empty stomach was not likely to contribute to the steadiness or clearness of the intellect during the morning, and in almost every case it lay the foundation of future mischief; for so habitual did it become, that the soldier felt that without the accustomed stimulant nothing could be enjoyed. The appetite for the morning meal, paralysed by the previous night's excess, was by this means re-excited, while the desire for more, and an eager longing for the accustomed canteen hour, followed as a matter of course.

In tracing the causes which have obtained for the Anglo-Indian soldier such a bad pre-eminence, it would not be fair to overlook the almost total want of society, excepting of course such as is to be found within the limits of a military cantonment. Nothing can be more monotonous or oppressive than a state of existence like this to any one possessing an idea beyond the performance of an unvarying routine of military duties. Amongst the great variety of characters that a regiment includes, there are always some to be found of a stamp superior to the rest—some who have, perhaps, been forced into their present circumstances by the pressure of unavoidable misfortunes, the faults of others, or indiscretions of their own.

Many I have known whose high talents and gentlemanly manners have not prevented them from falling into the depths of infamy and vice, whose consciousness of their own abilities has only added a double bitterness to their already humiliated condition, and whose superior acquirements,, when joined to low and depraved habits, have only rendered them more odious and contemptible to their comrades. Still more numerous are those who, neither possessed of education nor abilities, have nothing to regret in the choice they have made, but who, for these reasons, are not, perhaps, the less qualified to make excellent soldiers. Amongst such a medley a man may obtain companions enough, but society—the companionship of the contented and cheerful spirits that make up the pleasant circle of an English fireside forms no feature in Indian life.

Amongst the many cases which I might select in illustration of the foregoing observations, that of a young man named Blake, strikes me as particularly deserving of notice. This person had received a good classical education, and combined with it, a perfect knowledge of several modern languages. He had been originally destined for the medical profession, but owing in all probability to his own misconduct, found himself at the end of his studies in the situation of a private in a dragoon regiment. He was a fine athletic young fellow, and well versed in his military duties, but his temper was passionate and vindictive, and at those periods when he was under the influence of liquor, he became a raging devil.

His abilities might have procured him promotion to the rank of a non-commissioned officer, had he any ambition that way, but he appeared to entertain a contempt for the grade, as was natural enough for a man who had fallen from a higher station. Perhaps his real motive was distrust of his own temper, and if so, he acted wisely, for in no situation in life are the patience and good feeling of a man so constantly put to the test, as in that of a non-commissioned officer.

By one of those strange circumstances so frequently observable in dispositions like Blake's, he had formed a close intimacy with a young man belonging to the same troop, whose character was directly the reverse of his, and it was a matter of surprise and remark to their comrades that a friendship between individuals of such a different stamp should be so long kept up. At length, however, a quarrel, produced by some sudden ebullition on the part of Blake, took place, and a serious rupture was the consequence. The latter swore he would be revenged, and the means he took to accomplish his purpose were as diabolical as they were consistent with his previous character.

On the evening previous to the period which he had fixed for the execution of his project, he was observed to be more than usually excited, and to pay frequent visits to the canteen. Having spent all the ready money which he possessed or could contrive to borrow, he disposed of his books to his comrades for the purpose of raising more. By this means he kept up the fearful state of excitement which must have been necessary to the contemplation and execution of his infernal designs.

Early next morning, when the troop to which he belonged fell in, for the purpose of field exercise, Blake was reported absent. Little notice was taken of the circumstance at the time, it being conjectured, from his behaviour of the preceding evening, that he had made his way to the native *bazaar*, which was a favourite place of resort with him.

As the regiment was about to return from field drill, word was brought to the commanding officer that the body of a dead soldier had been discovered, in a dreadfully mutilated state, in a *nullah* or ditch, a few hundred yards distant from the horse lines. The discovery had been made by some of the native followers, on their way to the forage yard.

The corpse was found lying on one of the banks with a pistol firmly grasped in the right hand, which bore the marks of having been recently discharged. But for the uniform and the number of his forage cap, which too plainly indicated who the unfortunate suicide was, no one could possibly have recognised it as that of Blake. The whole of the upper part of the skull and face was literally blown away, and presented a most shocking appearance. The remains were immediately conveyed to the hospital and deposited in the dead house, to await the necessary investigation,

On stripping the body, a paper addressed to the commanding officer, was found, and in this document were detailed, at considerable length, the pretended reasons which had induced him to put an end to himself. He accused himself of having committed a degrading offence, and charged the young man with whom he had been so long on terms of intimacy, with having participated in his crime. He alleged that remorse and shame had so worked upon his feelings that he could no longer bear the burthen of a disgraceful existence, and had consequently resolved upon destroying himself!

Such a charge coming from one who was about to appear before the awful tribunal of God, and who, not content with destroying his own hopes of salvation, endeavoured, by the solemnity of a last declaration, to effect the ruin and blast the reputation of a virtuous and estimable young man, whose only crime appears to have been, his allowing himself to be drawn into an intimacy with such a character, was so revolting and incredible, that I need not say it was treated with utter contempt and disbelief.

It could not fail, however, to wound the feelings, and affect the peace of mind, of the individual charged, although both his comrades and officers testified to him, in every possible way, their commiseration and sympathy. He was shortly after promoted to the rank of a non-commissioned officer, a reward not only merited by his undeserved sufferings, but by his undeviating good conduct and strict performance of his duties.

The corpse of the wretched suicide was borne to the grave, not in the usual affecting manner in which the remains of a brave soldier are carried to their last resting place, but by the hands of natives of the lowest caste, and ignominiously interred without the precincts of consecrated ground.

Before I quit this subject, I cannot pass over another sad instance of perverted talents which fell under my observation. The person to whom I allude was a man who, like Blake, had moved in a respectable sphere of life previous to his entering the army, and who had recourse to drink, to drown the consciousness of his own degradation. In spite of this failing, however, his natural abilities obtained for him the rank of sergeant, and he even filled a staff employment at the period of which I speak. Notwithstanding the repeated scrapes into which his favourite propensity betrayed him, and the as frequent admonitions which he received on the subject from his superiors, he yielded to it more and more, until a serious breach of discipline brought him before a court martial, by which he was sentenced to confinement in the *congee* house, or, as it is termed in the regiment, the "Cocked hat." To such of my readers as are not acquainted with the nature of this punishment, a short description of it may prove interesting.

The *congee* houses constituted a quadrangle of strong cells, built in ranges, one above the other; and were entered by means of balconies. Each cell was about eight feet high, and eight by four square, and confinement in this narrow space, joined to the overpowering heat of the climate and scanty allowance of bread and water served to the inmates, rendered the punishment in the case of a man labouring under the debilitating effects of *arrack*, equivalent to a sentence of death. In fact four men lost their lives in them subsequent to the circumstance I am about to relate, and the cells were abandoned as a place of punishment.

The poor sergeant, on being introduced into one of these dark holes, made the observation that in case the means were within his reach, he would destroy himself sooner than remain any time in it. His excited manner left but little doubt as to the seriousness of his purpose, and the sergeant in command of the guard resolved to leave no instrument within his reach by which he might be able to effect it. On searching him, he found a pair of cotton heel-ropes, such as are generally used to secure the troop horses when standing in their lines, and also a razor and common table knife, both of which articles were properly forbidden to prisoners.

As he was about to remove them, the prisoner suddenly attacked him, and endeavoured to regain possession of them. Finding the sergeant too strong for him, he made a sudden rush past him, and overthrowing the sentry, down the staircase, rushed out of the building. A general chase now commenced; the fugitive clearing the enclosed space, bounded across a prickly pear hedge and ran towards the river, shouting and screaming like a madman. A short space more would have sufficed to enable him to gain the river and terminate his career by a plunge, when he fortunately stumbled, and fell. His pursuers were upon him before he could collect himself for a fresh run, and he was immediately restored to his cell.

During the night he kept up a constant uproar, and it was evident from his wild and idiotic chattering that the unfortunate man was fast losing his reason. Towards morning, the noise abated a little, and the sergeant again visited his cell. What a spectacle met his eye! Pale, haggard, and with eyes starting out of their sockets, the wretched man looked as if he had passed through a long and wasting illness. He talked wildly and incoherently, and there was no longer any doubt of the hopelessness of his case. He was removed to hospital without further opposition on his part, for his strength appeared to be completely exhausted. The utmost attention was, of course, paid to him; but he never recovered his senses, and death soon after put a termination to his sufferings.

About this time, two non commissioned officers, who held situations of considerable responsibility, were brought to trial for conduct justly deserving punishment, *viz.*:—defalcations in their troop accounts; and what aggravated the offence on the part of one of the accused was, the discovery that he had, for some time, carried on a wholesale and systematic plunder of the dead. This latter charge must not, however, be taken too literally, as it simply means, the giving in false returns of the effects and credits of a soldier deceased, in order to defraud the relatives, who, in the event of no will having been made, are entitled to claim the amount. Frauds of this nature are of frequent occurrence in India, and are regarded with a severe eye by the military authorities.

After an investigation in which both charges were clearly brought home to the prisoners, they were found guilty, and reduced to the ranks, the most culpable being sentenced to five hundred lashes, and the other to three months' solitary imprisonment. Such a disgraceful fall could not but prey heavily on the minds of the unfortunate men who had hitherto borne irreproachable characters, and had served several years in the regiment. One died shortly afterwards from fever, brought on by excessive drinking, and a broken heart terminated the existence of the other.

CHAPTER 7

I Hear a Confession

I could have smiled to see
The death that would have set me free.

Of all punishments prescribed by the articles of war, I know none which strikes the mind of the soldier with so much terror as that of solitary confinement. The lash, severe and disgraceful as it is, and even death itself are considered far preferable; and with the knowledge of this fact, it is surprising that men should be found to object to the amelioration of our criminal code by the abolition of capital punishment. If prevention be the policy of the law, and not punishment, then, I say, let that system be adopted which is calculated to make the most lasting and terrible impression on depraved minds, and you will do more to check the spread of crime than all your melodramatic executions have hitherto effected.

Criminals, who can look calmly upon death, and who have no belief in a future state of punishment and reward, cannot contemplate, without horror, the prospect of being shut up for life in company with their own guilty thoughts, and of being rendered powerless as regards the gratification of their passions. The state of inaction to which the vicious energies of such beings are condemned, by solitary confinement, is a moral death in itself infinitely more fearful to them than physical extinction.

Of the extent of this feeling I had frequent opportunities of judging while we lay at Kaira. Scarcely a day passed without the occurrence of courts-martial, too frequent held for the investigation of charges unworthy the notice of such a tribunal, and at most deserving only a slight reprimand. Here let me bear testimony to the great improvement that has taken place of late years in this respect. Owing to the judicious instructions issued in 1834, by the late Lord Hill, these inquiries are now only instituted in cases whose magnitude calls for solemn investigation. The consequence is, that the tribunal itself is regarded with a greater degree of respect, and its decisions are not subjected to the injurious interpretations which were formerly put upon them. At the period at which I write, courts-martial were but too frequently made instruments of tyranny, on the part of the subordinates in command, and many an act of grave oppression was cloaked under their authority.

It was during the period when the regiment was in the field at Cutch Bhooj, that three privates were sent down from that place to Kaira, to take their trial on a charge of robbing a public tumbrel containing specie for the payment of the troops. A general line court martial was assembled to investigate the matter, and the evidence adduced was, as nearly as I can recollect, as follows. The tumbrel, which stood close to the guard tent, was forced open during the night, and treasure to a considerable amount abstracted. Several pieces of coin were observed scattered about in the sand in its vicinity, and a portion of the bottom of the vehicle having been forced inwards, it was not difficult to conclude how the robbery had been effected.

Three of the guard, who had relieved each other during the night as sentinels at the tumbrel were discovered in the morning in a state of intoxication, and though none of the missing treasure was found upon, them, it was clear that if the robbery had not been committed directly by them, it must have been effected through their connivance. After a lengthened investigation, the court found all three guilty, and sentenced them to a year's solitary confinement, which in such a climate as India, and with the severe dietary regulations then in existence, was nothing short of a slow and torturing death.

On the day when the sentence was to be publicly announced, the regiment was ordered under arms on the parade ground in the rear of the barracks, and the culprits were led into the square. Whilst the adjutant was reading the finding of the court, the countenances of two of the prisoners became ghastly pale, but that of the third assumed a daring and impudent expression. Coolly unloosing his jacket and stock, and flinging them on the ground, the latter stepped forward and addressed the commanding officer.

"Flog or shoot me at once, your honour; but do not condemn me to the Cocked Hat. Five hundred lashes—anything would be better than that."

Such a breach of military discipline as this rarely occurs. We watched the result with breathless interest.

The colonel, retaining his self possession, replied sternly, and without the least appearance of excitement in his manner,

"Put on your jacket instantly."

"It is horrible to condemn a man to a lingering death like that," rejoined the prisoner. "I will cheerfully undergo any other punishment you may award me, but do not send me to the *congee* houses."

Major B——," said the colonel, "if that man again refuses to obey, instantly run him through the body."

The officer addressed advanced towards the refractory culprit, and stood prepared to execute the orders of his superior.

"Put on your jacket this instant, or abide the consequences," again cried the colonel, in a voice which rang through the parade ground, and found an echo in every man's heart. We knew him too well to doubt that he was in earnest.

The prisoner remained motionless for a few seconds. The pause was one of intense interest to the bystanders. The fellow was known to be a daring and reckless character, and it was just a tossup which of the alternatives he would accept. He at length put an end to our anxiety by stooping down and picking up his clothes, muttering at the same time something about the hardship of his case.

"Silence, you scoundrel," exclaimed Colonel W——, "I have not done with you yet. For this mutinous conduct you shall have to answer when the term of your imprisonment (of which you shall not be spared one day) shall have expired. Your present behaviour shall form subject for inquiry before another court martial, and you, major, will select whatever evidence may be necessary."

The prisoners were then removed to the *congee* houses, but as the regiment left Kaira before the term of their sentence had expired, they were conveyed to the fortress of Ahmednuggar, to finish it there.

Immediately on their liberation another court of inquiry was called for the trial of the soldier who figured in the above scene. He was sentenced to three hundred lashes; but in consideration of the long confinement he had already undergone, and the favourable report made of his conduct whilst in prison, his other offence was forgiven on condition of his publicly begging pardon in presence of the assembled regiment.

One of the other two, whose general conduct had always been equivocal, and who had not the credit of possessing very nice powers of discrimination where property was concerned, was soon after brought before another court martial, on a charge of peculation. This fellow was an Irishman, and possessed no inconsiderable share of the humour which characterizes his countrymen. Notwithstanding the exhibition of great skill and natural shrewdness in his defence, poor Pat was unable to convince the court of his innocence, and was condemned to the triangles. Being a small man, and of a spare and delicate habit, we expected that his physical powers would have succumbed under the punishment.

Not so, however, he not only bore the lash without wincing, but between each round administered by successive operators was ready with some absurd remark, which converted the whole scene into a farce, rather than an example, neither officers nor men being able to preserve their gravity. Amongst other things he had the assurance to tell his commanding officer—"that he might release him, as he had now been thrashed to his satisfaction." Like a skilful player, however, he reserved his best stroke for the last, for as they were casting him off from the triangles he turned round, and with a countenance in which fun and suffering were ludicrously blended, exclaimed—"Ah, you may talk of tobacco, but this is the real twist."

I have elsewhere alluded to the reputation for unhealthiness which Kaira has always enjoyed amongst the military stations of India, and I shall now have occasion to bear testimony to its truth. The cholera broke out in the month of May, 1826, and it immediately spread amongst the Europeans with the desolating rapidity of the plague. Notwithstanding the efforts made by the medical men to arrest its progress, it swept away hundreds of the regiment, and universal gloom and consternation prevailed. The majority of the officers, with the exception of the colonel and a few others, fled to the Presidency, and the desertion of our superiors only added to the general despair.

Out of the sixty men who generally occupied each of the barrack rooms nearly the whole were consigned to the hospital or the grave, and the few that remained either awaited their turn in hopeless despair or endeavoured to drown their sense of the impending danger in mad intoxication. Like the skeletons at the Egyptian feasts a wasted and debilitated form but just escaped from the claws of death might occasionally be seen presiding at these fearful debauches, the revellers in the inconsistency of their terrors at once dreading and courting familiarity with the object of their fears.

I for some time escaped the influence of the contagion and was accordingly selected to perform the duties of hospital orderly. Being of a naturally strong constitution I undertook this dreaded office with less apprehension than others, and to this feeling I attribute my having so easily escaped the disease as I have invariably observed timidity to be a strong predisposing cause of it.

The scene that presented itself when I entered the ward assigned to me, was however calculated to shake the strongest nerves. From thirty to forty of my comrades lay either writhing in the agonies of death or in a state of hopeless prostration. The temperature, owing to the excessive heat of the weather, and the crowded state of the apartment, was absolutely suffocating, and joined to this a peculiar and most disagreeable odour, such as usually proceeds from animal substances in a state of putrefaction, prevailed throughout the wards and passages. Agonizing groans and cries everywhere saluted the ear, and wherever the eye fell it was shocked by the blue or livid hues which mark the phases of this terrible disease..

On some natures, hardened by familiarity with human suffering or brutalised by indulgence and excess, spectacles like these either produce no effect or afford subject for drunken ribaldry. I turned away in disgust from the hospital sergeant—an over-fed ignorant clod of a Yorkshireman, as he observed on inducting me in my duties, "Here you sir, here are six foxing chaps to take care of, they are all croakers so, you mustn't humour them too much."

On making a round of the patients entrusted to my charge, I was struck by the appearance of a young man named Whelan, a native of Ireland. He had been counted one of the finest men in the regiment, his figure being a model of manly beauty, and his strength herculean. He was evidently near his end, and I was struck by the wild and horrified expression which lit up his ghastly features.

"Whelan, my poor fellow," said I, "is there anything I can do for you?"

"Yes," he exclaimed seizing my hand with a frenzied grasp. "You can get me a priest: for the love of God fetch him instantly, for there is something on my mind which I wish to confess before I die."

"I fear it will not be in my power to comply with your request, as there is no Catholic priest to be had here. The Rev. Mr. Payne who is now in the other ward, will however pray with you should you desire it."

"No! no! not for the world," screamed the dying man, "do you think I want to turn heretic—the priest—the priest—as quick as you can, or it will be too late."

Having pacified him by promising I would endeavour to procure one, I left him for a few minutes, and sought out Mr. Payne. Having called him aside, I communicated to him my suspicions that Whelan had something of a startling nature to disclose, adding at the same time, that as the dying man was a Catholic, I was afraid he would not accept his services.

The clergyman appeared struck with what I told him, and hastening to Whelan's bed, began to impress upon him mildly, the necessity of preparing himself like a Christian for the solemn change that was about to take place; when the wretched man exclaimed with a terrific oath, "that no Protestant parson should come near him." Mr. Payne endeavoured to reason him out of this resolution, but finding it in vain withdrew.

I remained at the bed side for some minutes in silence. The invalid lay motionless with his face buried in his hands.

"William," he suddenly exclaimed in a tremulous voice, while the tears streamed down his cheeks, "for the love of the virgin mother of God, fetch me a Catholic priest. I cannot die contented until I see one."

"If there is one to be had in the neighbourhood rest assured he shall be brought," was my reply. "Here is the doctor, so I will now leave you for a while, and see what is to be done."

At this time there was only one Catholic priest to a district comprising two hundred square miles, and he was a Portuguese, speaking but a few words of English. The Rev. Mr. de Souza, the gentleman in question, resided at Kaira, which was several miles distant from the barracks, and he could only come over every third or fourth Sunday to perform divine service. As the ritual was entirely in Latin and Portuguese, the worthy clergyman might as well have remained at home for any spiritual benefit the soldiery obtained from his instructions. The only advantage they might be said to have derived from his coming was their being spared the drill to which they were subjected under a broiling sun, while we Protestants went to church.

It has often occurred to me that a government, professing to be paternal, and which has made some advances towards toleration, ought not so long to have overlooked the religious disadvantages under which the Catholic soldiery labour in India. It is, I know, customary to argue that so long as there is a national church, it would be dangerous to its interests to take any step which might imply a recognition of the rights of any other establishment, and our sensitiveness and jealousy on this point has been ludicrously exemplified in the use made of Lord Ellenborough's famous proclamation respecting the Somnauth gates. There may be force for aught I know in the arguments used against the appointment of catholic chaplains to the troops in India; but at all events, there is not much consistency, for we endow a college for the education of Catholic priests, and yet refuse their aid where their services might be most beneficial to the state.

The veneration in which the lower orders of the Irish hold their pastors is proverbial; and I have no hesitation in saying that their admonitions would have more effect in restraining the excesses of the Catholic soldiery than the severest military enactments. It is hard, indeed, that the poor soldier who has braved the dangers of war and climate, in the service of his country, and who yields at length to their effects, should, in his last moments, be denied the only consolation that can render the termination of his career a happy or contented one. Christianity claims the Catholic as well as the Protestant amongst her children, and it would be well for the sentimental piety which groans and turns up its eyes at highly drawn pictures of Hindoo ignorance and Suttee superstition, and which sends out missionaries at vast expense, to convert an unwilling people, if it would turn a look of commiseration on the state of religious destitution in which the poor Catholic soldier finds himself in India.

To return from this digression, as soon as I had obtained leave, I despatched a messenger to Kaira for Mr. De Souza, requesting his immediate attendance, as it was uncertain whether the sick man would survive the night. The reply was, that the clergyman was ill, but would come over in the morning, if able to do so.

I returned to my charge, and found him asleep. The doctor had given him a composing draught, but informed me there was little or no chance of his recovery.

At nine o'clock the disease reached its crisis, and the patient sank rapidly; he inquired despondingly if there was any chance of the priest's arrival. I communicated to him the reply I had received from Mr. De Souza.

"It will be too late," groaned the unfortunate man. "This is terrible, to die like a hound by the roadside, without absolution for one's crimes, or even a word of hope to cheer one's last moments."

" Come, come, my poor fellow," said I, "you must not give way to despair like this. God is merciful, and will pardon those who are sincere in their penitence. A contrite heart is always acceptable to Him, even though it may not be sanctified by the forms of the church."

"Oh, that I could think so. There are some crimes that an eternity of suffering cannot expiate."

"Listen to me, Whelan, and weigh my words well. The mercy of the Almighty is infinite, and there is no offence in his eyes so great as not to admit of atonement. If your contrition be full and sincere, there is room for hope, even though it manifests itself at the eleventh hour."

"I would willingly believe you; but my heart tells me that mine is a crime which can never be forgiven."

"I do not want to force myself on your confidence, but I should be better able to advise and console you were I made acquainted with the cause of your despair."

"It would frighten and shock you," was his reply. "I dare not communicate it to you, and yet I feel it would relieve my mind of some portion of the fearful load which is weighing it down. And after all," he muttered to himself, "what have I now to dread from its disclosure. I have nothing more to fear on earth."

A pause of a few minutes succeeded. The invalid raised himself on his elbow with an effort, and casting an anxious and inquiring look towards the beds of the other patients, motioned to me to stoop towards him. His eyes glared with a wild and unnatural fire, and the violence of his emotion became so great, that after twice trying to speak, his voice only became audible in a hissing whisper.

"I am a murderer," was the brief, but terrible import of his communication. I bounded to my feet horror stricken, and notwithstanding the spirit of Christian charity which had dictated the few words of consolation I had addressed to him, it was some minutes before I could regain myself possession, and venture to look again towards him. When I did so I found that he had sunk back upon the bed exhausted, and from the drawn and livid appearance of his features it was evident that the hand of death was upon him.

"I knew that there was no hope for me," he despairingly exclaimed us he watched the result of the internal struggle, which this dreadful disclosure had occasioned in me."

"Think not so," I replied, when I observed the effect which my agitation had produced upon him. "I have already said that the mercy of God is as boundless as his power. Your crime is great, but if your repentance be proportionate, there is no ground for despair."

"Thanks, thanks," he faintly ejaculated, "your words bring comfort to my heart. Sit down beside me, and while I have strength left I will tell you my story."

Painfully as my curiosity was excited, I begged of him not to attempt it in his then state, for I saw that the slightest further effort would only accelerate his end.

"You must hear the particulars now," was his reply, "for fearful as has been my crime, I do not like to leave you under the impression that it has been committed in cold blood, or with any base or sordid design. You must know that I am the son of a respectable farmer in the South of Ireland. I was educated for the priesthood, but feeling that I had no vocation for the profession, I returned home from college and took the superintendence of my father's farm. I had not been long installed in my new duties when I fell in love with the daughter of a small shopkeeper in our neighbourhood of the name of Lanigan, and being young and tolerably good looking the feeling was soon returned by the girl.

"The match was approved of by the parents of both, and but a few weeks were to elapse before the marriage, when one morning a labourer who worked upon my father's farm came and informed me that Mary and her father were playing me false, for they were encouraging the addresses of another suitor of the name of McDonnell, who had just come from America on a visit to his family, who were in the same class of life as ourselves. My informant added that McDonnell had obtained old Lanigan's consent to take his daughter back with him to America by the promise of a loan of money to assist in extricating him from some difficulties he was in, and that the girl's head had been turned by the splendid promises he had made her.

"You may judge of the rage into which I was thrown by the baseness and perfidy of their conduct and seizing a stout cudgel I ran, or rather flew, to Lanigan's farm. My anger and mortification were in no way diminished on looking through the window of the little sitting room where the family usually passed their evenings, by seeing my rival with his arm round the waist of my promised bride. Bursting in the door, I suddenly stood before the affrighted group. The old man turned pale as a sheet, and trembled violently, Mary screamed and held down her head, while McDonnell appeared fidgety and uneasy.

"'Is this true, Mary?' I exclaimed. 'Can you be so lost to all sense of shame as to break your plighted troth and give me up for a stranger? Is this a dream, or am I to believe the evidence of my own eyes?'

"Mary sobbed but ventured no reply.

"'And you are a party to this Lanigan,' I said turning to her father after a short pause. 'Mercenary old fool that you are, you have sold your own and your daughter's honour to the first comer, who gave you your price. Were it not for your grey hairs, I would teach you what it is to break faith with an honest man.'

"'It seems to me, young gentleman,' sneeringly interposed Me Donnell, who had evidently screwed up his courage, and was determined to brave out the matter, 'that you are not a very welcome guest here, and I therefore advise you to take yourself off as speedily as possible.'

"'Scoundrel,' I exclaimed. 'How can you face the man you have so deeply injured, and add insult to your other villainy. Out of my way this instant, or I will brain you on the spot.'

"'Two can play at that game, my young game cock, so bottle your anger, and take your pretty face to some other market, or I may spoil its beauty.'

"This was too much. With a blow of my cudgel I stretched the fellow lifeless on the earth. The blood streamed in torrents from his nostrils, and Mary threw herself screaming on his body. I rushed from the house.

"Late that night I received notice that the officers of justice were in pursuit of me. McDonnell was dead, and I was a proscribed murderer, with a price set upon my capture.

"Obtaining a little money from my father, I proceeded as quickly as possible to Dublin, and from thence crossed the channel. Finding a regiment on the point of embarking for India I enlisted in it, and have by that means succeeded in escaping detection. I have not however been equally successful in drowning the stings of conscience. Sleeping and waking the bloody features of Mc Donnell have been always present to me, and remorse has rendered my life insupportable. The first ray of hope or comfort that has since dawned upon me has been drawn from your words, and I feel now as if my heart was relieved from a portion of the weight that has so long oppressed it.

"I thank you from my soul," added the poor fellow, grasping my hand fervently; "you have divested my last moments of a portion of their bitterness, and I have only one request more to make of you. Under my head you will find a prayer book, given to me at parting by my poor mother. Should you ever return to England forward it to her, and tell her that wicked and thoughtless as I have been, I have never parted with her last gift, although I have made but a sorry use of it. It will I know gratify the poor old woman, and afford her some consolation for the loss of an unworthy son."

"I am glad, for both our sakes, that you have made this disclosure to me," was the observation I made when he had concluded. "Your first avowal left a painful impression on my mind, but it has been in some degree removed by the facts you have just communicated to me. Although it is a fearful thing to take the life of a fellow creature, the degree of criminality attaching to the act must, of course, depend on the circumstances under which it has been committed. Smarting under the sense of one of the greatest injuries that can be inflicted on one, and provoked almost to madness by the insulting conduct of a successful rival, some excuse may be made for the hasty and unpremeditated crime into which you were betrayed. I dare say that at the time, you had no more serious intention than to inflict summary chastisement."

"Examining my own feelings at the time impartially, I am afraid that I cannot thus easily acquit myself. My evil passions had become so excited, that I felt my rival deserved to die upon the spot, and I fear that the wish was but father to the act. I am not sure that it was not even resolved upon before I entered Lanigan's house."

"I should hope not, Whelan, for much of one's accountability, for acts such as these, depends on the degree of premeditation with which they are committed. Let me, now, take this prayer-book of which you speak, and read a portion of its contents to you. There is nothing which so composes and tranquillizes the mind as prayer."

Taking the volume, I read several of the beautifully worded and impressive passages with which the Roman Catholic ritual abounds, and I was rejoiced to perceive that they produced a soothing effect on his mind. He at first shed tears, but gradually became calmer, and it was evident he was more at peace with himself.

"Are you inclined to sleep?" I at length inquired, shutting the book. "If you will try and compose yourself to rest, it will, perhaps, do you good."

"I feel a sense of drowsiness stealing over me. Draw the covering over my shoulders, and I may perhaps sleep awhile."

I did as he requested, and went to attend to my other patients, whom I had wholly forgotten in the interest excited by his narrative. When I returned to his bedside, the poor fellow was dead.

Chapter 8

Proceed to Kirkee

Some men employ their health, an ugly trick,
In making known how oft they have been sick.

I was at length attacked by the epidemic, but thanks to the strength of my constitution, it manifested itself in a modified form. Its effects were, however, so debilitating, that when the cantonments at Kaira were broken up, I was sent to Bombay with the sick, whilst the remainder of the regiment proceeded to the Deccan.

It was now the month of September, and though the heat of the season had in some degree abated, the sun was still powerful. We proceeded in *doolies* to Cambay, which was about three day's march from the hospital, and were there embarked in a number of small and rudely constructed boats, having a covering of bamboo rods, stretched loosely along the gunwale, so as to form a sort of temporary deck. Owing to the deep mud which lined the banks of the river, we could only get to the boats on the shoulders of the natives, and in some instances they missed their footing, and capsized us. Ill and exhausted as we were, these accidents did not the less afford us subject for banter and amusement.

Nor did our mishaps end here. In the hurry and confusion of embarkation the medical stores were forgotten, and even water became scarce. The individual deemed himself fortunate, who was able to procure a cup-full from the native boatmen, who gave it reluctantly enough, owing to repugnance of caste. They invariably break the vessel which has once been touched by European lips, and this prejudice occasioned a most distressing scene on our passage. Two of my comrades, who lay stretched in the agonies of death in the hold of one of these little vessels, vainly endeavoured to reach a small brass bowl which happened to lie at a short distance from them. Through anxiety to possess themselves of the prize, and jealousy of each other, neither could reach it; so they rolled about in a firm embrace, uttering fierce threats and imprecations. The native boatmen looked on unmoved at this painful struggle, and did not make the least attempt to assist them.

The bodies of several of our unfortunate comrades were committed to the deep, during the passage through the gulf, but in consequence of the insufficiency of the measures taken to sink them, they were carried after us by the tide, and were to be seen constantly floating round the boats. A trooper and his wife died raving mad, cursing each other in their last moments in the most horrible manner. Several hours' interval occurred between their deaths, yet, singular to relate, although the body of the man was flung into the sea early in the morning, and that of the wife not till the afternoon, they were found floating side by side, the same evening. The superstitious discovered in a circumstance simple and natural enough in itself a fruitful subject for their sage speculations.

The influence of the sea breeze soon began to manifest itself in the improved condition of the sick. The convalescent felt an increase of strength, the desponding began to hope, and the dying to shew some returning symptoms of life. The run occupied about three days, and it was joyful news to all, when it was announced that the lighthouse of Bombay was in sight. On entering the harbour, we were disembarked at the Bundar steps, and immediately conveyed in *doolies* to the general hospital.

We found everything in a state of complete and comfortable preparation for our reception, beds having been made up for nearly three hundred men. A transition from the hardships we had lately undergone, to the comforts of an establishment like this, soon produced the effects that might have been anticipated. Though some cases terminated fatally here, the unaccustomed comforts and able medical assistance, so liberally provided us, were unquestionably the means of preserving many a life that would have otherwise fallen a sacrifice.

As we improved in strength, we were drafted into the town barracks, a large building situated within the fort, where, in our early morning walks on the esplanade, we inhaled the fresh and invigorating sea breeze, and were, in a few weeks, completely restored to health. The regiment having by this time arrived at Pamwell, a town situated about seventy miles from Bombay, we received orders to repair to headquarters, and embarked for that place early in February.

My comrades having been, for a considerable period, deprived of their usual allowance of spirits, some of them procured a few bottles of it the evening previous to our departure, in order to make merry during the passage; but, alas! how delusive are the pleasures of hope. The basket in which the precious cargo was deposited did not escape the vigilant eye of our worthy chief, who demolished its contents with a kick, during its transit from the beach to the boat, while the disappointed owners, knowing well that remonstrance or grumbling would only add to their offence, were but too glad to disclaim all knowledge of the interdicted liquor.

We accomplished the distance from Bombay to Pamwell in little better than twelve hours. After leaving the harbour, and coasting along the shore to the south for a league or two, we entered the Pamwell River, the scenery of which is extremely beautiful. Winding through a richly wooded and mountainous country, and broken at intervals by small islands clothed with verdure, this fine river presents at every turn an ever varying succession of delightful views. As its waters begin to narrow, you catch sight of the ridges of some lofty mountains which form part of the stupendous *ghauts*, a passing gleam of sunshine occasionally gilding their rugged tops, or penetrating the obscurity of their tremendous ravines. Here and there may be seen a towering and detached peak—whose cone, wooded to the summit and crowned by the lofty and feathering palm, casts its long shadow over plains covered with rich fields of grain, and dotted with smiling villages.

There is always something gratifying to one's feelings in the prospect of an approaching reunion with friends. After an ordeal such as we had passed through, in which uncertainty prevailed as to who had escaped or fallen victims to the terrible visitation by which we had been afflicted, it was not surprising that our arrival at head quarters should have been regarded with more than ordinary interest. For our own parts we were but too well pleased to escape the nostrums of the doctors, and the dietary regulations, not to look forward to this meeting with equal eagerness. We disembarked at Pamwell, at an early hour of the morning, and were immediately surrounded by our good natured comrades, who shook us warmly by the hand, and inquired with affectionate interest after those who were missing. Alas! there had been fearful ravages made in our ranks, and many a poor fellow might be seen turning away with a tearful eye, as he received the news of the loss of an old friend or brother in arms.

We found a capital breakfast prepared for us by the thoughtful kindness of our comrades, I do not think I ever made a meal in my life with so much relish, so excellent a sauce is a hearty welcome on the part of one's entertainers.

Pamwell, if we are to judge from the antiquated appearance of its buildings, must be a town of very old date, and though it is not considered a place of commercial importance, it possesses a numerous population. It is situated on the great road leading to the Bore Ghauts, and forms the direct medium of communication with the Deccan country. These advantages, joined to the convenience of its spacious Bunder, to which boats of the largest burthen can come up from Bombay, afford support to its inhabitants without the necessity of exerting themselves in home production. Excellent inns and taverns are to be found here, and the traveller, whom business or amusement induces to visit the Deccan, will readily find conveyances to all parts of it. A stage coach has been lately started between Pamwell and Poona, and although the fares are high the speculation has been found to answer extremely well.

After remaining about three weeks at Pamwell, the regiment proceeded by detachments to Kirkee. Having ascended the *ghauts*, we halted for a day on a sort of natural platform, formed by the junction of two immense rocks. Here an adventure occurred which caused us some alarm.

The *ghauts* it is well known are infested with tigers, which though of a smaller species than those of Bengal, are not the less dangerous to encounter. The natives often fall victims to their rashness in venturing across the mountain tracks without being properly armed, and so frequent became accidents of this nature, that it was found necessary to post up a government notice, in the Hindostanee language cautioning travellers not to quit the high road.

Undeterred by this warning, three of our men determined to ascend the stupendous hill that overlooks the Lover's Leap, a deep ravine gained by a pathway winding down the other side of the mountain, but which is rarely frequented, from its being known to be a favourite resort of these animals. Having toiled up to the brow of the declivity, it was proposed that they should descend into the ravine, but two of the party showed the white feather, the dark and suspicious aspect of the chasm beneath not being of the most inviting character. The third remained firm to his original intention.

Claridge was the name of this man. He was brave to temerity, and once he had taken a resolution there was no shaking it. He took his gun, and having seen to the priming of it, prepared to descend the mountain, after making an engagement with his comrades that he would meet them on the same spot in an hour.

Having wandered about during the interval, in search of game, his companions returned to the place where they had appointed to meet him, but he had not as yet made his appearance. They waited some time; but at last got impatient, and began hailing him from different points, in the hope of making him hear, but all their efforts proved fruitless.

They now became really alarmed, and held counsel as to what was to be done. Their fears prevented them from descending into the ravine and satisfying themselves at once, and the only alternative that remained was, to return to the camp and inform their officers of the circumstance. As soon as the facts were stated to the colonel, he lost no time in procuring the assistance of a number of *waggries* or beaters, men trained from infancy to hunt down and exterminate the tiger. Mustering about forty in number, and carrying torches of pine and bundles of dried grass, for dusk had now set in, they proceeded to the spot, accompanied by a number of soldiers with loaded fire arms.

Having been shown the spot where Claridge had descended, the leader of the *waggries*, a grey-headed, but powerfully built Mussulman, shook his head significantly.

"Quick," said the colonel, observing his indecision. "The man may be lost while you hesitate."

"*Allah* is great," was the reply, "and he only can save your comrade. I know the place well, *Sahib*—it is full of tigers, and I wouldn't descend into it for fifty gold *mohurs*."

"Burn them out, then," exclaimed an old pensioner, who had lived for some years on the *ghauts*. "It is the only chance the poor fellow has."

Some bundles of lighted grass were, accordingly, thrown into the *nullah*, and on its catching the dry brushwood, the whole ravine was soon enveloped in flames. The spectacle was magnificent, for night had now set in, and the red tints reflected back from the charged atmosphere, invested the wild scenery around with new and still more imposing features.

We held our breaths in the intenseness of our anxiety, and not a sound was heard, except the occasional roar of one of the wild denizens of the jungle, who, driven from his lair by the flames and smoke, gave vent to his rage in terrific bellowings. The flames spread with extraordinary rapidity, the ravine being choked up with weeds and light brushwood, and as they cleared away the obstacles to our view, we could penetrate, at a glance, its deepest recesses.

"A purse of gold," shouted the colonel, "to the first man who descends and examines the *nullah*."

Several of the soldiers started forward, and were on the point of diving down the precipice when they were restrained by a loud exclamation from the old beater, who was at the head of the party, and who pointed eagerly to a part of the jungle which he had been for some time attentively examining by the light of the flames which were rapidly advancing towards it. We ran in a body towards the spot, where he stood, but our eyes not being so practised as his in this sort of work, we could at first observe nothing.

"In the tall tree to the right, immediately under that jutting rock, do you not see a dark form," said the beater impatiently.

"I see nothing," replied the colonel, "your eyes deceive you."

"I am no child, *Sahib*, to mistake a *wag* for an *adammy*. That is your comrade, and he will be lost if some effort is not immediately made to release him from his present situation. In half an hour more he will be surrounded by the flames."

"Then let us descend at once to his assistance," cried the colonel. "Who will accompany me."

"Hold," cried the old Mussulman, in a tone of authority. "Are ye all mad, or tired of your lives. Remain quiet, and I will save him."

Calling two of his men aside, he conferred a few moments with them. Then taking a strong rope, and descending the hill to the right, so as to skirt the jungle they were presently lost to view. In a few minutes more they were again visible at the opposite side of the ravine, immediately above the rock which projected over the tree to which our attention had been called.

This rock formed a sort of natural platform, or shelf about ten feet in length and extremely narrow, but the descent to it was precipitous and dangerous, and could only be attempted by those who were practised mountaineers, and had confidence in their own skill. The distance was only twenty feet, but so steep was it that the least error in calculation or accidental slip would have precipitated the whole party into the fearful abyss beneath. Laying hold of the stump of a tree which grew on the brow of the declivity, the leader of the party hung suspended in the air while his companions glided one after another down his body, the second man grasping firm hold of his feet, and affording support to the third in his turn. This feat, of course, could only be effected by great nerve and bodily strength. Securing a firm footing on the ledge of rock the last descended served as the base of this human ladder, while the remainder of the party made good their descent.

Having spent a few seconds in examining their position, a rope was tied round the waist of one of the party, while the other two, by one of those ingenious contrivances which are often resorted to by mountaineers, formed a sort of windlass of the stump which had helped their descent, and gradually lowered their companion. We watched their proceedings with the greatest interest, for we could not but perceive the risk they ran, and at length had the gratification of perceiving the beater ascending from amidst the clouds of smoke, which were drifted down the ravine, with the body of our insensible comrade in his arms. A loud cheer burst from us at this glad sight, and in a few minutes the poor fellow was placed in safety on the summit of the hill. He was half dead from fright and suffocation, and was immediately conveyed to the camp in a litter. He was, however, soon restored, and his adventurous spirit received a check from the circumstance, which proved of no small advantage to his subsequent career.

Starting at three o'clock next morning, we arrived at Carlee, about seven, and as soon as the tents were pitched, I availed myself of the opportunity of visiting the celebrated eaves of the same name, which are situated about three miles from the village.

The approach to the spot is by a narrow and difficult pathway, winding round the sides of a steep mountain, and for the most part concealed or choked up by weeds or brushwood. The caves, of which there are several formed one above the other, are hewn out of the solid rock, and are situated about eight hundred feet above the level of the plain. They are profusely ornamented with sculptures from the heathen mythology, which have considerable merit as works of art.

The visitor at first passes through a mean and ruinous temple, dedicated to the Goddess Siva, which forms the principal entrance to the excavations. Here he is received by a set of naked but merry urchins, who beset him with importunate offers of service, reminding one forcibly of the good-humoured perseverance of the Irish guides.

On entering an inner chamber we saw some beautiful columns, having capitals shaped like a bell, surmounted by elephants, with intertwined trunks, and bearing groups of male and female figures.

I made some inquiries of an old *faquir*, who was seated in this chamber, respecting the foundation of the temple, but the only thing I could collect from the confused mass of tradition with which he overwhelmed me was, that the name of its builder was King Poondoo.

Immediately over the entrance, at a considerable height from the platform on which we stood, were some eagles' nests, one of which contained a noble bird. The men who accompanied me threw stones at her in order to dislodge her; but their efforts proved fruitless, as the majestic-looking creature appeared to look down upon them with contempt, and to regard the huge flints which assailed her on every side as so many pebbles.

Exasperated at her indifference, a man of the name of Fulton, determined to ascend to the spot, and put her to flight. Throwing off his jacket, and arming himself with a stout cudgel, he climbed to a ledge of rock which overlooked the nest, and commenced belabouring the bird with all his force. Unaccustomed to such rough usage, the eagle flew out, and flapping its huge wings in his face, deprived him of sight and tumbled him down the precipice. He luckily fell on the platform, and thus escaped being dashed to pieces, which he certainly would have been, had he missed it; but he was so much bruised and injured by the fall, that we had to carry him in a sort of litter to the encampment, where it was some time before he recovered.

A few marches more brought us to Kirkee, the new headquarters of the regiment. The barracks were not as yet completed, and we were obliged to continue under canvas for nearly four months.

The monsoon set in this season with great severity. As early as the month of May the sky began to threaten an unusual fall of rain, an indication termed in these parts the *Elephanta*, and which generally precedes as well as terminates the rainy season The prospect of being exposed to the fury of an Indian season while under canvas was anything but agreeable, and many a longing eye was directed towards the barrack which was now beginning to assume a somewhat regular and habitable appearance.

If there be any one thing more trying than another to the temper of the soldier, it is the necessity of living under canvass. There is no season of the year that has not its attendant miseries; alternately starved by the cold, or broiled by the rays of a tropical sun, subjected to a close and uncomfortable association with a variety of characters not always the most obliging or agreeable, and brought into perpetual collision with petty interests and jealousies, I know no situation in life which puts one's patience and forbearance so severely to the test,

But in a monsoon season these miseries are doubly aggravated by circumstances perhaps trifling in themselves, but presenting such a perplexing combination of annoyances, that it requires more than an ordinary share of philosophy to bear up against them. Numerous reptiles infest the ground under and about you—there is not a stone or blade of grass in your vicinity which does not conceal a lurking foe in the shape of the centipede, or the still more venomous scorpion, whose sting is not easily to be forgotten, while myriads of buzzing insects dispute your meals with you.

In short there is hardly a redeeming feature in that unenviable state of existence denominated a camp life. All is crowd, bustle and confusion—you have not a spot which you can call your own—not even the narrow space which you lie upon—and the pleasurable sensation of being suddenly roused from sleep by the falling in of the temporary fabric above your head, and finding yourself immersed in mud and water, while your traps are perhaps making an excursion of some hundred yards from their owner, is but a mere trifle in the everyday life of a soldier while in the field.

That which annoys you most perhaps, is the fact that these mishaps produce no relaxation in the responsibilities of your situation. The morning appears calm and smiling, and the disasters of the night are forgotten. The field day must be attended to as if nothing unusual had occurred—your arms and accoutrements, though mixed pell-mell with the debris of the demolished tents, and scarcely distinguishable from the mud in which they are embedded, must be sought out, and restored to their usual pipe-clay order. Duty, stern and unrelenting, admits of no excuse, and the soldier must fall into his ranks at the general parade call as if he had passed his night in calm and refreshing slumber.

It was after such a night as this, when our tents lay prostrate on the ground, and the camp presented a scene of unparalleled confusion, in which it was difficult to say whether the ludicrous or distressing predominated, that we received the long expected order to pack up and prepare for the occupation of our new barracks. The river Moola had become swollen to an unusual height, and it became doubtful whether our troops would be able to cross the bridge which separated the encampment from the cantonments. This bridge was situated about half a mile from where we lay, and was the only spot where the river could be passed. It was constructed partly of stone and partly of wood, the centre arch being elevated about sixty or seventy feet above the bed of the river. So high was the then state of the flood, that the water was dashing over the middle arch, while the rush on the banks was tremendous, the surrounding country being inundated for miles round.

The camp followers having been ordered to cross first, it was with considerable difficulty they were induced to attempt it. Composed of motley groups of men, women and children of all countries and castes, and having in their trains as curious a variety of conveyances, their passage was not unattended with interest Cooks laden with culinary utensils—*dobies,* or native washerwomen, mounted on, or driving before them their buffaloes; *ghorrawallas* leading asses, on which were seated groups of chattering urchins, and *hadjims,* or barbers with their large shaving boxes, and girdles stuck round with razors, followed each other in slow succession, and with evident anxiety and trepidation. Nor was their alarm entirely without cause, for several narrowly escaped being washed away by the flood.

One poor woman, with an infant in arms, had reached the centre of the bridge, when finding the water ascending above her knees, she lost her presence of mind, and letting her child fall, it would have been swept into the current the next moment had not a stout *bheesty,* who happened to be near her, caught the falling infant, and with one hand placed it on the leathern bag of his buffalo while with the other he supported the fainting and terrified mother, and bore them both in safety to the extremity of the bridge.

As the troopers were crossing the bridge, three a breast, the horse of a man named M'Donald became frightened, and suddenly rearing, backed against the slight wooden parapet of the bridge, broke it with his weight, and was precipitated into the stream with his rider. The man was an excellent swimmer, and managing to disengage himself from the animal, contrived to land in safety lower down. The horse was however lost.

The cantonments at Kirkee presented at that time a very different appearance from their present improved condition. Not a vestige of a road was then to be seen, and our cattle were up to their saddle girths in mud, as we traversed the distance from the bridge to the barracks. But insufficient as the buildings, and other accommodations prepared for us, proved, we felt but too thankful to have the protection of a roof over our heads, and to exchange the damp ground for the luxuries of a dry floor and comfortable cot.

Our cattle, however, did not appear to be of the same opinion, for the night being again stormy they broke from their fastenings in the barrack yard, and galloped back to the old encampment. How they contrived to re-cross the river without accident is surprising, for the flood did not abate till late on the following day. Finding the usual commissariat allowance was not forthcoming they were soon glad to return to their quarters, and it was not a little amusing to see these animals straggling back to their lines after the lapse of two or three days, completely subdued in spirit, and following each other with a docility which nothing but their tired and exhausted state could have produced.

The custom of living with native females in a state of concubinage is a practice notoriously prevalent amongst the European soldiery in India. In most military cantonments a spot adjacent to the barracks is set apart for the erection of huts for the accommodation of those who feel disposed to enjoy the pleasures of a Benedict's life without any of its annoyances. This place is designated, in the language of the country, *the patchery*, and the occupants are permitted to furnish their own mess like married soldiers. That such a mode of life is anything but conducive to the welfare of the soldier will hardly admit of dispute. It is, however, sanctioned in too many instances by the example of his superiors; and I do not remember ever to have heard this glaring breach of morality denounced by the lips of the preacher.

Surely such a wide field for practical instruction should not be left uncultivated. When we regard the physical as well as moral degradation likely to arise from this depraved state of existence, it is not too much to say that it is the duty of the philanthropist, but more especially that of the ministers of religion to combat the evil wherever it is to be found, and to impress on persons in authority the necessity, if not of suppressing it, by restrictive measures but at all events of refraining from sanctioning or encouraging it themselves.

Such connexions, the result of passion (for it would be absurd to give it any other designation) on the one hand, and of purely interested motives on the other, cannot be otherwise than productive of ruin and debasement to those who form them. The attractions of the native females are considerable, and the influence, I might even say the tyranny which they exercise over their infatuated victims is such as to mar or effectually destroy the usefulness of the young soldier; nor is youth alone the sufferer. The old stager whose head has grown grey in the service, and whose experience might be supposed to have taught him wisdom, is but too frequently the slave of their seductions.

A numerous offspring is, perhaps, the consequence, and the father is thereby deprived of all hope, or even wish of returning to his native country. He has either formed ties which cannot be readily broken off, or from long association he has become so identified in character and habits with the natives, that he has no longer any desire of escaping the state of degradation into which he has fallen. Results like these are deeply to be deplored, whether we regard their effect on public morality, or the discipline of the service; and it is a great pity that the authorities should either wink at them, or afford them encouragement in their own persons.

A tragical incident, arising out of this anomalous state of society, occurred shortly after our arrival at Kirkee. A man of the name of Cooper was selected as an assistant to the waiters of the officers' mess, and this employment necessarily brought him in frequent contact with the native women usually attached to these establishments. Amongst the latter was a young female of great personal attractions, and Cooper had not been long acquainted with her when he took her into keeping as his mistress. The lady, though she lived on the resources of her new lover, saw no necessity for complying with the advice of the song, which recommends that the old one should be first discarded, and accordingly bestowed her favours with equal impartiality on one of the native waiters in the establishment.

On discovering this fact Cooper became furious, and determined to take a signal revenge. Borrowing a fowling-piece under pretence of enjoying a day's shooting, a practice common amongst the dragoons, he watched his opportunity, and as his unfortunate rival was in the act of depositing some dishes on the floor of an outbuilding adjoining the mess-room, he fired at him through an open window and shot him through the head.

The report of the gun brought a crowd immediately to the spot, and a strict search was instituted after the murderer. No person had witnessed the act, but the discharged gun lay outside the window, and it was immediately recognised as that which Cooper had borrowed.

The officers and the regimental sergeant major immediately proceeded to his quarters, and found him in bed, feigning profound sleep. He was ordered to arise, and dress himself, on which he betrayed symptoms of alarm, and on being questioned relative to the soiled appearance of his clothes, but more particularly his shoes, he gave a confused account of himself. It should be mentioned that this occurred during the monsoon, and a great deal of rain having fallen his footsteps had been traced to his barrack room from the window where the murder had been committed, and on comparing his boots with the fresh imprints, they were found to correspond. He was immediately placed in a *congee* house for greater security, and two sentinels with loaded firearms were stationed at his door. An investigation of the affair took place the following day, and the necessary evidence having been collected he was sent under a strong escort to Bombay, and turned over to the civil authorities.

During the interval that elapsed between his apprehension and final trial, the conduct of this man was characterised by the most heartless indifference, which might in some degree be attributed to the notion, at that time prevalent among the European soldiery, that there was an unwillingness on the part of government to proceed to extremities against them where the crime affected the native population only. How this absurd and mischievous idea got abroad I am wholly at a loss to conceive, but the result of it nevertheless was, to invest the trial of this man with a degree of interest which it would not otherwise have excited.

Various were the speculations afloat as to the line of defence likely to be adopted against evidence, circumstantial it is true but yet so conclusive, that no one could entertain a moral doubt as to the guilt of the prisoner. A feeling of jealousy was known to have existed on his part against the deceased—the gun had been borrowed and prepared with an evident and deliberate intention, and seen in the possession of the accused a short time previous to the murder—it was found on the spot from whence footsteps corresponding with the size of the prisoner's boots were traced to the barrack room in which he slept, and the confused account which he gave of himself when awakened from his pretended sleep, formed altogether as complete a chain of circumstances as it was possible to link together.

To the indictment, when arraigned, the prisoner pleaded not guilty, and when the evidence was gone through, to the astonishment of every one present, he acknowledged his having shot the man, but asserted that his death was purely accidental, as the piece had gone off whilst he (the prisoner) was in the act of cleaning it. He accounted for his subsequent conduct by the alarm which he felt at the chance of the accident being misconstrued, and a serious charge brought against him.

Strange as it may appear, this defence, perhaps the best which could have been suggested by the ingenuity of counsel, might have been the means of saving him, if he could have proved that he had made a similar statement previous to his trial, and could produce any one witness in support of it. This chance was offered him, and had he only been aware in time that it would have been afforded him, it is not improbable he might have procured someone who would have got him off by hard swearing.

It was necessary however that the party to whom the communication had been made, should be named at once. This was a poser, which even the fertile resources of his counsel could not relieve him from, and the jury, after a brief but emphatic charge from the learned judge, brought in a verdict of guilty. He was sentenced to be executed in front of the jail at Bombay, and met his fate with the same reckless indifference which he had betrayed throughout the whole of the affair.

Chapter 9

The Rajah's Entertainments

Il n'y a pas de meilleur soldat que l'homme ennemi de l'oppression.

It is contended that the severity which characterises our military enactments is essential to that perfect state of subordination which should prevail amongst properly organised troops, and it is not for me to dispute the assertion. I wish only to show that the arbitrary powers placed in the hands of our officers to effect this object are but too frequently abused, and that individuals are sacrificed in order to attain it. To those who are in the habit of looking beneath the surface of things, it may not be uninteresting to know that the stern and rigorous rules of military discipline are partial in their operation, and that there is a large amount of silent, but undeserved suffering amongst the great body of the soldiery, who have neither the right to complain against, nor the power to resist, the wanton tyranny to which they are subjected.

It is customary in the army to perform the barrack room fatigue duty by rotation, one or two men as the case may be, being daily required to clean out each of the rooms, or perform other necessary duties connected with them. A portion of their time is employed in carrying the messes from the cooking house to the rooms, and for this purpose the orderlies, as they are termed, fall in, and are marched under the command of a non commissioned officer to the former, a few minutes before the bugle sounds for dinner.

It one day happened that a dragoon named Kennedy, known by the *soubriquet* of "Knowing Joe," was amongst the persons called upon to perform this duty. This man belonged to a class of persons generally denominated amongst us, military lawyers, fellows who contrive to breed a good deal of mischief, and who are particularly obnoxious to the authorities. He had got involved in various scrapes from time to time, but owing to his superior tact and cunning, had generally contrived to escape punishment. His turn, however, came at last, and that too for an offence which was far from proportionate to the punishment meted out to it.

On the orderly men falling in previous to marching off for fatigue duty, Kennedy was reported absent. A moment after he made his appearance, and stated that he was going to wash his hands at the pump at the rear of the barracks, not more than a few yards distant, when he would return and join the party.

"Fall in immediately, sir," shouted the corporal, a tyrant in his petty way, and known to have an inveterate dislike to Kennedy.

"When I have washed my hands," was the reply of the latter, as he ran to perform his ablutions.

This was all that passed on the occasion. The vindictive corporal immediately placed him under arrest, and a court martial having been called next day to investigate the charge, unfortunate Joe was found guilty of a breach of discipline, and sentenced to three hundred lashes, which were duly administered in the riding school, in the presence of the assembled regiment.

Our worthy commandant wound up a long lecture, which he delivered on the enormity of the offence, by the following injudicious, and undignified remarks:—

> And now, sir, I have long waited for this opportunity of teaching you better manners and a proper respect for military authority. You are well known as an old, and, I fear, incorrigible offender, and are sufficient to spoil the younger soldiers in the regiment by your example. I will teach you and all who hear me, that fatigue is a duty, and a very important one too. I trust this will be a warning that you will recollect to the latest hour of your existence. Take him down.

How far the punishment inflicted was in proportion to the offence, or the allocution justified by the occasion, I will leave others to judge, This much I may be permitted to observe, that had the culprit been any other than poor Joe, the offence would, in all probability, have been overlooked or treated as a joke. I admit that in a depot where there are generally to be found characters of the lowest and most motley description, and these too, principally composed of young men, but recently subject to the bonds of military restraint, a certain degree of strictness, perhaps more than is generally observed with the older members of a regiment, may be necessary. But it may be fairly questioned if scenes such as I have described are not rather calculated to strike the young soldiery with disgust and hatred, than to impress them with a high notion of the justice or impartiality of military legislation. This I know that desertions have been but too frequently the result of them.

Another exemplification of the manner in which "the little brief authority" of the army is abused, will be found in a circumstance that occurred to myself. It is, or at least was, in those days, the practice on a Saturday afternoon, as a relaxation from the ordinary routine of drill, to give over the garrison to the quartermaster and his subordinates for fatigue duty. The men were told off in parties some to assist in cleaning the barrack yard, some in making roads or wheeling gravel, and others in exercising their taste for horticultural pursuits in the commandant's garden. Some of duller capacity had easier tasks assigned them, such as cleaning windows; and others, luckier still, were set to clean the knives and forks or the boots of the sergeant-major and his wife.

To my lot fell the window cleaning, and it so happened that a pane of glass, which had been previously cracked, in the sergeant-major's window, gave way while I was in the act of rubbing it, and fell to pieces on the pavement. This was certainly no fault of mine, so I duly reported the accident, and at the same time pointed out the state of the window when I commenced my task. The sergeant said the thing was impossible—he could not have mistaken the original condition of the sash, nor was the evidence of the other soldier who was employed in the same room with me deemed worthy of the slightest credit, A non commissioned officer is never known to fall into error, but more particularly in a case where the acknowledgment of the fact in dispute may be attended with expense to himself. The pane was smashed and I was the delinquent, or at all events I was the party selected to make good the damage,

As a preliminary step, and to record how impartially justice was administered, it became imperative upon me to go down to the quartermaster's office, where a book was kept in which all deficiencies or repairs chargeable to the soldier were duly registered, and to which he was required to affix his signature as a voucher for the correctness of the claim. This was too much not only to compel me to pay for damage which I had not occasioned, but to place upon record my having done it. I considered it a duty to resist, and flatly refused to comply with what I could not help considering a most impudent attempt at imposition.

I was immediately ordered to hold myself in readiness to appear before the commandant at the office, and was shortly after brought before him. Having stated the grounds on which I declined paying the demand, and expressed a hope that he would not enforce it, I was not a little confounded by the reply which I received.

"So you persist in refusing to pay for the glass which it appears was broken by your carelessness. You have been long enough in garrison to know better; but if you are still ignorant of your duty, I must endeavour to teach you. Mr. M'C——," he added, turning to the adjutant, "have the goodness to direct the trumpeter to sound orders, and let a garrison court martial be immediately assembled. You shall have the justice of your case investigated as fully as you can wish, and it will be *my* duty to see the decision of the court carried into effect whatever it may be."

The conclusion of the sentence was uttered with a significance that left little doubt on my mind as to what the probable result would be, and I now felt anxious to back out of the affair as quickly as possible. In this I was assisted by the adjutant, who had himself risen from the ranks, and who, notwithstanding some little eccentricities of character, was, on the whole, a good natured and well meaning man. Observing me completely crestfallen, he remarked to the commandant that being but a very young soldier, I might possibly be ignorant of the danger I incurred by my refusal, and at his request I was again afforded an opportunity of recalling it.

Perceiving no alternative, and having the recent affair of Kennedy before my eyes I was but too glad to avail myself of it, and consented that the damage should be set down against me in my monthly account. The commandant drily observed to me, "I am glad that you have at length come to your senses. I will overlook your conduct for once, but take care that you are not again brought before me while you remain in this garrison."

Comment on these cases would be superfluous; yet they form but "trifles light as air," in the category of military abuses, which my memory recalls at this moment, and which I cannot help thinking might be remedied without detriment to the discipline of the service. Respect for authority can only be ensured by convincing those in subordinate stations that it is exercised with impartiality and discretion. This rule applies to military as well as civil life, and were it more frequently acted on in the former, I have no doubt that the service, as well as the individual, would be materially improved.

The strength of the regiment having been greatly reduced by the mortality which lately prevailed amongst us, no time was lost in reinforcing it by large drafts of men from England. News having been received at head quarters that a body of recruits, amounting to one hundred and eighty-five men, had just arrived at Bombay, a detachment, in which I was included, was immediately despatched to the Presidency for them, together with a few recovered men who had been left in the hospitals.

We remained but a short time at Bombay, and it having been determined that we should return to our cantonments by land, we reached Baroda in the latter part of September.

Baroda is a rich and populous city, situated about two hundred and eighty miles north of Bombay and fifty due east of the gulf of Cambay. It is the capital of the petty monarchy established in Guzzerat by a chief of the Guicowar family, who, at the head of an army of Mahrattas in the pay of the then reigning sovereign of Sattara, invaded and plundered Guzzerat in the early part of the eighteenth century. The population amounts at present to upwards of two hundred thousand.

One of the most conspicuous objects in the town is the house of the resident, Mr. Williams, which is built in the English style and surrounded by handsome gardens, bearing evidence to the liberal mind and cultivated tastes of the proprietor. Mr. Williams is a keen sportsman as well as a skilful horticulturist, and numerous are the stories current of the feats he has performed

Shortly previous to our arrival, several of the inhabitants of a village called Myee, about sixty miles from Baroda, came in and reported that a large tiger was infesting the surrounding district, and that during his nocturnal visits he had killed and carried off several children. The alarm became so great, that the inhabitants began to desert the place, none of them being hardy enough to face him. The moment the resident heard of the circumstance, he determined on extirpating this terrible animal, and taking his native servant, Abdallah, who generally accompanied him on expeditions of this nature, he rode down to Myee the following day.

Having put up at the village for the night, the two adventurous sportsmen sallied out early next morning, armed with spears and double-barrelled guns, and plunged at once into the jungle where the animal was supposed to have his lair. A deep growl soon indicated where he lay, and Abdallah, taking a circuitous route, gained a *nullah* unobserved by the tiger, and thus placed him between them.

Taking a steady aim from his lurking-place, Abdallah fired, and wounded the animal in the throat. The tiger bounded towards the spot from whence the shot proceeded, and the servant pulled the trigger of his second barrel. The gun missed fire, and flinging it aside, he coolly received the enraged animal on his spear. Mr. Williams had by this time come up, and discharging both the barrels of his gun, laid the tiger dead at the feet of his servant. One of the balls unfortunately glanced off a tree and buried itself in the shoulder of Abdallah. The poor fellow swooned away, from the loss of blood, and hastily binding up the wound with his handkerchief, Mr. Williams returned to the villagers for assistance, which was readily and gratefully afforded him, the object of their terrors having ceased to exist.

Abdallah recovered from his wound in a few weeks, and was the narrator of the story. He exhibited to me, with no small degree of pride, the skin of his formidable adversary, which is to be seen amongst various other relics of the chase, in the hall of the Residency.

Orders having been issued by the *rajah* that the short sojourn of the detachment at Baroda should be rendered as agreeable as possible, various sports and athletic feats were got up for our amusement. An elephant fight was fixed for the day succeeding our arrival, and having been long curious to witness a spectacle of this sort, I made my way about five o'clock in the morning, to a large plain in the vicinity of the town where it was announced to take place.

Here I found an extensive arena dug in the ground to the depth of from twelve to fourteen feet. On each side two small chambers, accessible only by a narrow aperture, were excavated so as to afford temporary shelter to the *chures* or criminals, engaged in this combat, in case the elephant should push them to extremities. Over the entrances to these chambers were suspended the arms of the *chures*, which consisted of two spears, a bow and arrows, a piece of red and white cloth, about three yards in length, and a shield of highly burnished steel, with coloured devices in the centre.

At the western extremity, and close to the very edge of the arena, stood a platform gaily decorated with drapery of various colours, and crowned by a gilt canopy, containing a splendid velvet ottoman fringed with gold lace, and having four enormous tassels of the same precious material. This was the *rajah's* seat, and immediately on the left were placed two chairs for the resident and his sister, a young lady about nineteen, and possessed of great personal attractions. To the right were the places allotted to His Highness's son and ministers.

About six o'clock the discharge of artillery and the discordant music of the native bands in His Highness's service announced the approach of the *rajah*. By this time the sides of the arena were thronged by thousands of turbaned spectators, but owing to the kind precautions of our princely entertainer a place was set apart for the Europeans, and we enjoyed the spectacle without being crowded, or in any way inconvenienced.

On the *rajah* taking his seat, the sable multitude made the usual obeisance, while the Europeans uncovered, and received His Highness with other marked demonstrations of respect. Silence having been proclaimed, four criminals were brought into the arena, heavily chained, and they were asked by the *rajah* whether they preferred death by strangulation to taking their chance of an attack from such savage beasts as he chose to let loose upon them. Desperate as it was, they of course preferred the latter alternative; and their irons having been knocked off, and their friends permitted to speak with them, they were ordered to prepare for action, and to choose their weapons of defence and attack.

To Europeans unaccustomed to inhuman and brutalising scenes like these, the painful suspense which precedes the arrival of the ferocious animal which is to be made the instrument of death or torture, is nearly as great as to the criminals themselves. The principal actors in the scene are kept in ignorance until the last moment as to which of the brute tribes their fearful antagonist belongs, and it may well be imagined that their state of mind during this brief interval must be one of intense anxiety. So sensibly was this apparent to me, and so strongly were my own feelings moved, that I would almost have preferred being in the place of one of those poor devils, to remaining a passive spectator of such a scene. Shocked and disgusted, I would gladly have left the spot, had the crowd which blocked me up on all sides permitted me to do so.

It was reported amongst us that a tiger or leopard would be let loose instead of an elephant, but this notion was soon put an end to by the appearance of a fine young animal of the latter species, which was led blindfolded into the arena. At first young Chung was not to be moved, but stood majestically regarding the vast multitude by which he was surrounded. One of the culprits commenced pricking him with his spear, while another tormented him by dancing the coloured cloth before his eyes, and the animal becoming enraged, at length turned suddenly on one of his assailants, who had barely time to evade him by darting into one of the chambers above described. He then gave chase to another, who avoided him with great nimbleness, and being driven mad by the joint attacks of his four persecutors, the sport was at its climax, when an accident occurred which added an unexpected and fearful interest to the scene.

Two opulent natives, who had possession of the inner seats, not being satisfied with the view they enjoyed, pressed forward in the excitement of the moment to the edge of the arena, and being pushed by others behind, accidentally tumbled in. The elephant instantly espied them, and, making for the spot where they lay prostrate, crushed one of them to death and tossed the other high in the air, his lifeless body falling in the midst of the gaping Mussulmen, and bruising several in its descent. The sun being now at its meridian the *rajah* ordered the sport to be put an end to, and His Highness having, to their great joy, pardoned the criminals, retired with his attendants from the scene.

On the following morning the sports were renewed with wild rams, who, after inflicting some severe contusions on their assailants, were despatched, and a tiger substituted in their place. The latter had been recently caught, and though not full grown, was strong and healthy. He was brought into the arena in an iron cage on a cart, the keeper being mounted on the top of the former, so as to let go the fastenings of the door at a signal from the *rajah*. Two athletic young men, who had been condemned to death for a murder committed in one of the neighbouring villages, were led in heavily chained, and their fetters being knocked off, they were directed to furnish themselves with the necessary weapons, and to prepare to defend themselves. Each man took a spear, shield, and dagger, and the other preparations being completed, the tiger was let loose.

On bounding from his cage the animal stood still for a few moments in the middle of the arena. A stuffed goat was thrown in to him, but he detected the cheat at once, and walking two or three times round it, lay quietly down at a little distance. The men were ordered to attack him, and the foremost launched his spear at him, which grazed the beast's shoulder, and had the effect of thoroughly rousing him. Uttering a deep growl, he bounded to his feet, and sprang on his assailants.

The man who had wounded him with the spear, and who displayed extraordinary coolness and presence of mind throughout the affair, received him on one knee, his body being protected by his shield and his right hand prepared to strike him with a dagger when a favourable opportunity offered. The tiger precipitated himself upon him with his whole weight, and laid him prostrate on the earth with his shoulder blade broken by the blow. The furious animal was about to make quick work of him when a well directed arrow struck him in the head, and penetrating the brain, stretched him lifeless beside his intended victim. The wounded man was then removed, and the *rajah's* pardon accorded to him and his companion.

Satiated with spectacles of blood, we left Baroda after a sojourn of about ten days, and resumed our route through a country presenting a delightful variety of scenery and extremely fertile. We reached the city of Broach after a pleasant march, and encamped on the northern bank of the Nerbudda.

Chapter 10

Mrs B——'s Ghost

Roving as I rove,
Where shall I find an end, or how proceed?
As he that travels far oft turns aside
To view some rugged rock or mouldering tower,
Which, seen, delights him not j then, coming home
Describes and prints it, that the world may know
How far he went for what was nothing worth.

One of the most singular institutions in the world is to be found here—namely an asylum for the reception of sick and infirm animals, and even the different varieties of the feathered and insect tribes are included in its benevolent provisions. This establishment is richly endowed, and the sleek Brahmins to whom the administration of the funds is entrusted show, in their own persons, that the comforts provided by the liberality of the deceased donors are not limited to the brute creation.

As might be expected from the character of the inmates, as well as from the well known habits of the keepers, the building appropriated to this purpose is filthy in the extreme, and requires no small degree of nerve on the part of a stranger to enter it. If his sense of smell be not over acute, however, and he is at all curious to see how association will soften down and harmonize the most antagonist instincts, the offence to his nostrils will be amply repaid by the sight of this collection. Here are to be found superannuated beasts and birds of every description, from the lion to the house cat, and from the eagle to the linnet, while rows of small boxes, ranged round on shelves, contain swarming multitudes of insects which are elsewhere regarded as the most troublesome and disgusting to the human race.

As I was leaving the hospital, I was forcibly struck by one of those strange inconsistencies which are calculated to disgust man with his species A wretched mendicant came tottering up to the entrance in the last stage of physical exhaustion, and implored relief. The Brahmins turned a deaf ear to his supplications, but a soldier who was with me, and who had more charity in his breast than these ministers of misplaced bounty, gave him a few *pice*. The poor fellow gratefully thanked him, and was proceeding on his way, when his strength failed him, and he sank fainting on the ground. The Brahmins no sooner observed this, than they surrounded the inanimate wretch and commenced picking off the vermin with which he was covered, to add to their live stock. We turned thoroughly disgusted from the spot.

As we are on the subject of misplaced affection for animals, I cannot help mentioning a circumstance that occurred while I was at Poona, and that occasioned me much amusement at the time.

I was one day sent to the lady of an officer, then on field duty, with a letter from her husband, which had just arrived by an orderly, and I was desired to ask if she had any reply to forward by the same opportunity, as the man was to start in a few hours. On arriving at her *bungelow* the letter was taken in to her, and I was kept waiting sometime in the ante-chamber.

I presently heard someone sobbing, and exclaiming in accents of heartfelt grief—

"My poor Mimi, my sweet pet am I going to lose you. Unfortunate woman that I am to be thus bereaved, one after the other, of all I hold most dear."

"Poor mother," said I to myself, "she is about to lose one of her children. There is nothing more admirable than a mother's love, nothing more touching than her grief."

"Please, sergeant," said an *ayah* entering the room, "my mistress begs you will sit down and wait a little: she is in trouble and can't see you just yet."

"Oh, by all means—child very bad—despaired of—?"

"Very bad indeed," replied the Abigail with a smile on her features. "Not expected to live another hour."

"A heartless jade that," was the reflection that occurred to me. "Had I not better leave my message?"

"Oh dear no—my mistress desires particularly to see you, and will soon be out."

Tripping out of the room with the most unconcerned air imaginable, she left me moralizing on the selfishness of human nature in general and of waiting maids in particular.

In the meantime the sobbing gradually ceased, and at the end of about a quarter of an hour Mrs. S—— made her appearance. Her eyes were red with weeping, and her whole appearance denoted the most profound woe.

"I regret having kept you waiting so long, sergeant," she said, "but I have been so engrossed in the sufferings of my poor little darling, that I have not been able to bestow a thought on anything else."

"Don't mention it, ma'am—hope he's better—sorry to see you in such trouble,"

"Trouble, sergeant, you can have no idea how my heart has been wrung. The prospect of losing a little angel, who has formed the solace and delight of one's existence is really dreadful to contemplate," and the flood-gates of the lady's grief were again let loose.

"It grieves me to see you take it so much to heart, ma'am. May I ask what is his complaint?"

"I really cannot tell, and this adds to my affliction."

"Can't tell, ma'am. Have you not sent for the doctor?"

"Why, to tell you the truth, I have not. The ladies of the regiment are so *very* fond of quizzing, that I am afraid to do so."

"Good God, ma'am, you surely don't mean that in a case like this you would be deterred from doing your duty by idle tongues."

"But I'm not sure that the doctor would come, sergeant, if I were to send for him."

"What the devil can all this mean," I mentally ejaculated, "this is the weakest minded of all the female fribbles I ever came across."

"Perhaps you will let me see your little patient, ma'am." I said after a moment's pause.

"By all means—step this way."

Leading the way into the drawing-room, the lady pointed to a bundle of flannel which lay carefully arranged on an ottoman, and stooping down I uncovered the contents.

I started back in astonishment at seeing, instead of a delicate infant, one of the smallest of all the diminutive varieties of the monkey tribe, to be met with in this part of India. My sensibilities having been previously worked up to the highest pitch, it may readily be conceived that the revulsion of feeling which I experienced, was as ludicrous as it was unexpected. Notwithstanding my respect for the wife of my superior, I became convulsed with laughter, and the irritated expression of her countenance so far from repressing, only increased my mirth.

"You forget yourself, sergeant," she at length exclaimed in an angry tone. "Your merriment is as unbecoming to you as it is insulting to me."

"I beg pardon, ma'am, but, the fact is, I mistook Jacko for one of the children, and am only laughing at my own mistake."

This excuse pacified her a little, and she begged that I would examine the monkey, and see if I could do anything for him. I found the little animal nearly lifeless, and could only recommend her to pour a little warm wine down his throat. This was immediately done, and Mimi revived, to the great delight of his affectionate mistress. On enquiring next day however I found the animal dead, and the captain's *bungelow* in mourning.

About two miles from Broach stands the celebrated *Bur* or Banyan tree, called by the natives Kiveer Bur, after the person who planted it. Some notion may be formed of the extent of this enormous mass of foliage, when I state that between three and four hundred natives constantly dwell under its shade.

Further down the river, on the opposite bank, stands a large *Sammy* house, or Hindoo temple, containing an effigy of Vishnu about four feet in height, the eyes of which it was reported were composed of two large diamonds of the finest water.

This rumour having, reached the camp, through the medium of some of the native followers who had been on a pilgrimage to the temple, a fool-hardy young fellow named Berry, who had been a working jeweller, determined to ascertain the truth of it. Being thoroughly conversant with the language and manners of the country, he succeeded in obtaining admission into the temple, and returned with word that the report was correct, and that the value of the diamonds could not be less than a thousand pounds each.

This excited the cupidity of the persons to whom he confided the result of his visit, and a plan was laid to rob the idol of its precious orbs. The parties of whom Berry made choice for his companions in this dangerous affair were Harvey, the man who has already figured in the commencement of these pages, and another unprincipled and reckless character, named Austin.

The night fixed upon for this daring attempt was that of Sunday. Having taken every precaution necessary to elude the vigilance of the sentries, and appointed the hour of midnight for a rendezvous, the three men stole out of the camp at different periods of the evening, and repaired to the spot agreed upon. Everything appeared propitious to their purpose, the night being extremely dark—(a circumstance of rare occurrence in this beautiful climate,) and the rain descending in torrents. It was not likely that on such a night the lazy priests would feel inclined to keep watch, or devotees to frequent the temple.

Having cautiously crossed the little wooden bridge which spanned the river, Berry advanced noiselessly to the temple, and ascending the broad steps that led to the entrance, cast a hasty glance into the interior. A number of lamps were burning in front of the idol, and the priests whose duty it was to watch over its safety lay buried in sleep on their mats, in a remote corner of the building.

The wind blew in fierce gusts through the trees which surrounded the temple, and the uproar of the elements was so great that it drowned all lesser noises. Satisfied with the result of his inspection, Berry returned to his companions, and a plan was agreed upon which was immediately put in execution.

The idol was hewn out of a solid block of stone weighing several hundred weight, and they were puzzled how to get it out of the temple without making such a noise as would have the effect of awakening its guardians. As to getting the eyes out where it stood it was out of the question, as the noise of the mallet and chisel would certainly be heard. Berry proposed that he should creep in on his hands and knees, from one of the side entrances and laying the idol prostrate on the pavement, tie a rope round it, so as they might draw it gently out without attracting the attention of the slumbering *faquirs*. The idea was excellent, and was as cleverly executed as planned. The deity was deposed from his shrine, and ignominiously dragged from his consecrated dwelling, and the only thing that now remained to be done, was to convey him out of the hearing of the inmates of the temple, so as to enable them to set to work with the hammer and chisel.

The veranda in which they stood was about forty feet from the ground, and it immediately overlooked the river. It therefore became necessary to lower the idol from the parapet by means of the rope, and to drag it across the bridge.

They had succeeded in accomplishing the former of these objects when they were suddenly interrupted from a quarter they least expected. A *faquir* who happened to be returning to the temple from the direction of the bridge, came suddenly upon them as they were trailing their singular prize after them, and was so struck with horror at this daring and impious act, that he stood staring at them in speechless amazement. Before he could recover himself, Harvey had seized him by the throat, and brandishing a knife threatened to stab him if he uttered a word. The frightened priest submitted quietly, and squatted himself in silent despair on the ground. Harvey was left to keep guard over him, while Berry and Austin dragged the idol across the bridge Into a field of *joharra*, where they proceeded to hew out the precious objects which were to reward all this labour and risk.

Much to their surprise they found that the eyes were moveable, and were only retained in their sockets by a spring. Had they been aware of this fact, what a world of trouble it would have saved them!

Cries of alarm were now heard in the direction of the temple, and it was evident the robbery had been discovered.

Knowing with what vindictive feelings the natives regard anything like insult to their religious prejudices, and having reason to fear from the approaching shouts which saluted their ears on every side, that they would soon be upon them, they dared not return to look for their companion, and accordingly left him to his fate. They succeeded in regaining the camp with their booty, but on proceeding to examine the value of it they discovered to their great mortification that they had been tricked by the *faquirs*, the diamond eyes being always removed at night and glass ones substituted in their stead.

In the course of the following day the dead body of Harvey was found on the banks of the river, the natives having massacred him where he stood, and mutilated his corpse in the most shocking manner. Not satisfied with this, the priests repaired in a body to the camp, and complained to our commander of the outrage committed on their temple. A reward of one thousand *rupees* was offered for the discovery of the other culprits, but without effect; they kept their secret until all danger attending its disclosure had passed away.

Leaving Broach we crossed the Nerbuddar, and after a couple of days march arrived at Surat. It is a large and well-built town, and carries on an extensive trade in cotton and ivory, the workmen in the latter article being considered the most ingenious in India. The fort is neither remarkable for its scientific construction nor strength; but it contains within its walls a neat little church, and a library for the use of the troops, which at this period consisted of only forty men belonging to the Honourable Company's foot artillery.

A singular custom of burying the dead prevails in this district. The corpse is covered with roses and fragrant herbs, and being placed on a bier, is carried in procession to the houses of all the relatives. On reaching each habitation the bier is lowered, and the attendants set up a howl resembling the Irish keen; after which the inmates come out, and embracing the corpse, strew more flowers upon it, and distribute coin amongst the attendants. Then falling into the procession, they proceed to the house of the next relative, where the same ceremonies are observed; and thus the funeral cavalcade continues to swell its ranks until it arrives at the banks of the river, where a pile of wood, saturated with ghee or oil, has been previously erected. The corpse having been divested of its silver ornaments is placed on the pile, and the latter being set on fire, is soon enveloped in flames. At a signal from one of the bystanders, the women who have been all this time closely hooded take their departure, and the men remain until the body is entirely consumed.

After staying here nearly three weeks, we proceeded to Kirkee, which we reached about the commencement of the new year, and were agreeably surprised at the improved appearance of the cantonments. The barracks had been completed, commodious stabling erected, roads cut in all directions, and various other steps taken to render them convenient and comfortable. It is astonishing what a revolution can be effected in a short time by the energy and industry of man.

We found the whole place in commotion owing to a frightful accident which had occurred just before our arrival, and which was attended with circumstances of rather a singular nature.

Amongst the ladies who had come over with us from England was the sister of a lieutenant of the second troop. She had not been many months at Kirkee, when she married an assistant surgeon belonging to the 19th Native Infantry, then stationed at Poona; but this did not prevent her frequently coming over to our barracks on a visit to her brother.

In these occasional trips Mrs. B—— was generally accompanied by the daughter of the adjutant of the same regiment, to whose society she had become extremely partial, and they spent much of their time wandering about the neighbourhood of the cantonments. The spots most favoured by them were the government gardens at Dapoolie, and a grave yard, romantically situated on the banks of the Moola. In this latter place there was much to captivate the fancy, and the associations connected with it only served to invest it with a melancholy sort of interest, that poetical and superstitious minds are generally susceptible to. Situated at an angle of the river, midway between the wooden bridge and a gentle cascade, which empties its waters into the broad stream; it commands several picturesque views, the value of which is enhanced by being seen at glimpses through the dense foliage of the grave yard,

Late one night, as Mrs B—— was returning to Poona in a buggy, driven by a native servant, she was overtaken by a storm at a distance from any place of shelter. Flashes of lightning, followed by loud claps of thunder and torrents of rain, soon rendered their situation most distressing, and to add to their alarm their horse took fright. The native driver—the worst possible dependence in such an emergency—lost all presence of mind, and with it all command over the animal. The horse bolted across a *nullah* into some cornfields, and overturned the vehicle, the unfortunate lady being thrown out and dashed against a tree, where she lay for some time insensible.

The driver who had only been momentarily stunned, endeavoured to restore his mistress to animation, but in vain. He then hastened to seek for assistance, and having with difficulty obtained it, had her conveyed back in this state to Kirkee.

On examining the injuries she had received, the doctor pronounced them so serious as not to admit of the slightest hope of her recovery. After the lapse of a few hours she recovered consciousness, and begged that her husband, who was on detachment duty in the Deccan, should be immediately sent for. Brain fever soon after set in, and it was evident that she had not long to live. An hour previous to her decease her husband arrived, and had barely time to receive the poor lady's last *adieus*, and to comfort her by an assurance, which she exacted from him, that her remains should be interred in her favourite graveyard, on the banks of the Moola.

As soon as the violence of his grief had subsided, he sent for a carpenter named White and gave him the necessary instructions for carrying his wife's last wishes into effect.

In compliance with another of her requests, the doctor gave orders that she should be interred in her bridal garments, and that her diamond ear-rings, and other ornaments, amounting in value to upwards of two hundred pounds, should be buried with her. The carpenter and his wife were the only parties, beside her brother, entrusted with the knowledge of this fact.

The heat of the climate renders immediate interment necessary after a decease, and there not being sufficient time to arch the grave over with brick-work, it was temporarily planked up for the night, White receiving instructions to procure some *gindy*-men, or native bricklayers, to complete the work next morning.

Now his wife, or the devil, or both, put it into White's head to rob the corpse of its valuable ornaments, by suggesting that it was a pity that so much treasure should lie buried uselessly in the earth, when it might be turned to some better account. The carpenter had always borne an excellent character previous to this; he was an old soldier, and had distinguished himself by his gallantry during the Peninsular war, as well as by his general good conduct. By a process of reasoning, natural enough perhaps to an ignorant mind like his, he succeeded in convincing himself that there could be no harm in taking, what was valueless and unprofitable to others; and this conclusion arrived at, he lost no time in carrying his project into effect.

Having communicated his intentions to a man named Macaulay, to whom he promised share of the spoil, it was agreed between them that after night set in they should meet at a place called "the Cobbler's fall," which was situated on the banks of the river at a short distance from the scene of operations.

The night was unusually dark, but flashes of lightning occasionally illuminated the atmosphere, and indicated the route. They reached the grave yard about midnight, and immediately set to work.

The planks were soon removed, and the carpenter proceeded to unscrew the lid of the coffin. They were busily engaged in this operation when a sudden noise made them both start to their feet. They peeped cautiously out. and hurriedly examined the surrounding objects.

A dark figure dimly visible in the obscurity of the night stood at a few paces distance, quietly regarding the grave. The fear of being discovered, and severely punished, was the first apprehension that flashed across their minds, but this soon gave place to superstitious terror on finding that this unexpected apparition preserved a death-like stillness, and continued to watch their proceedings in silence.

Both were stout hearted men as any in the regiment, but a guilty conscience will make cowards of the bravest, and they became so paralysed and helpless that they could neither satisfy themselves as to the reality of the object nor make an effort to escape.

This anxious state of suspense was at length broken by deep sobs, which seemed to proceed from the quarter where the figure stood. A sound resembling anything human proved a relief, even though it announced the proximity of a danger of a more material character than that which had previously alarmed them.

The carpenter and his companion felt that discovery was now certain, and crouching under the planks of the grave, they deliberated in whispers as to what was to be done. It was evident that the newcomer had not seen them, though the noise they had made might have reached his ears, and momentarily arrested his steps.

White was a quick witted fellow, and recollecting the fright he had received, he reflected that by working in the same way on the superstitious fears of their unwelcome visitor, they might be enabled to effect their escape.

Quick as thought he divested the corpse of a portion of its white habiliments, and wrapping them around him, popped his head through the opening which he had made in the planking of the grave, just as the unknown, satisfied the noise he had heard was a delusion, was about to approach it.

"Great God, is it possible?" exclaimed Doctor B——, starting back in consternation as the supposed figure of his wife rose slowly out of the grave, extending itself to a length which bore little proportion to life. "Speak to me, I beseech you, Jane, and tell me if there is aught that I have left undone which troubles your gentle spirit?"

The carpenter slowly raised his right arm, and extending it majestically towards the entrance to the grave yard, motioned the doctor to depart.

"Strange! most strange!" uttered the bewildered husband. "Am I dreaming? Again I implore of you to speak to me," he added, suddenly approaching the spectre, "and to tell me if there is any other wish of yours left unfulfilled."

"Begone," screamed the carpenter in tones intended for a sort of sepulchral mimicry of the female voice, but which were in reality tremulous from alarm.

"How can you thus treat one who has shown himself so devoted to you," continued the doctor pursuing the retreating ghost, and endeavouring to seize it in his arms. Instead of grasping thin air or shadowy form he found the portly figure of the carpenter in his embrace.

"Who the devil is this?" exclaimed the astonished doctor.

"It's me, sir—it's the carpenter," replied the trembling culprit.

"And may I ask what brought you here, Mr. Carpenter?"

"I came to measure the span of the arch, to prepare the woodwork for the bricklayers in the morning, sir."

"Indeed! and pray what is the meaning of all this white paraphernalia you have got about you?"

The carpenter, like all practised liars, did not stick at trifles, so he answered boldly.

"When I heard you entering the enclosure, sir, I thought it was someone coming to rob the grave, so I just put on a sheet to frighten them."

"A likely story, you lying thief, we'll see if you cannot invent a better one for the Court of Inquiry. Is there any one with you?"

"Only Macaulay, the smith, sir."

"And where is he skulking?"

"He's here, sir. Jem, come up, here's the doctor."

The smith dragged his slow length out of the grave, but did not attempt to utter a word in justification of himself.

The doctor ordered them to nail the planks down again, and as soon as they had complied with his directions marched them back to the barracks.

They were brought before a court martial on the following day and sentenced to 300 lashes each.

CHAPTER 11

Attacked by Arabs

Are all our braving enemies shrunk back,
Hid in the fogges of their distempered climate,
Not daring to behold our colours wave?

The *Rajah* of Kolopoor, a tributary to the Company, having in 1829 refused to pay up his arrears, Mr. Wilmot, the resident, left his territories, and it was resolved to despatch a strong force to bring him to reason.

Accordingly, in the month of September, a body of troops, consisting of two hundred of the 4th Light Dragoons, two troops of Horse Artillery, Her Majesty's 20th regiment of foot, one wing of the Queen's Royals, and several of the native corps, amounting in all to about five hundred men, left Poona for the scene of operations.

The weather was extremely favourable when we started, and we were all in high spirits, for this was the first time for several years that the Bombay army had been called into active service.

Crossing the *ghauts*, a short distance above Poona, we proceeded towards the bridge of Nara, a plain, heavy looking structure, spanning a deep and rapid river. To ensure the early arrival of the tents the following morning, it was determined to start them in advance of the main body, under the charge of a sergeant and twelve men, the non-commissioned officer selected for the purpose receiving instructions from the quartermaster-general's office, to proceed by a particular route, so as to reach the bridge by daybreak.

Instead of obeying these orders the sergeant thought fit to follow the advice of the guide, who suggested a nearer road, and proposed that they should ford the river at a place which he assured him was perfectly safe. The moon was shining in full splendour, and the sergeants had the satisfaction of seeing the whole of the heavy baggage passed over in safety. The men prepared to follow in single files, when the horse of a young man named Gawlay became restive, and losing his footing, was carried with his rider down the stream.

The sergeant quickly divested himself of his uniform, and plunged in after the unfortunate young man, but though he strained every effort to save him, the force of the current was such that he found himself unable to stem it. After an hour's fruitless exertion he returned to the ford in an exhausted and depressed state, well knowing that the responsibility of this unfortunate casualty would rest with him, and that he would be severely punished for the disobedience of orders which had occasioned it.

On the arrival of the detachment he reported the circumstance to the adjutant, and was immediately placed under arrest. A court-martial was held the following day, and he was found guilty on all the charges brought against him. The sentence was not proclaimed, but it was generally supposed that in addition to his being reduced, corporal punishment would be inflicted.

Being a young man of excellent previous character and high spirit, he determined that he would not submit to the disgrace of the latter. The night previous to the publication of the sentence he succeeded in making his escape from the guard tent, and proceeding to a *nullah* in the vicinity of the camp cut his throat with a razor. Some villagers, who happened to pass the spot next morning, found him lying in a pool of blood, but not yet dead. They conveyed him to hospital, but although the wound he had inflicted on himself was not a dangerous one, his mental sufferings were such that brain fever set in and carried him off.

We passed through Sattara on our road, and the *rajah* being friendly to us gave a *nautch*), or native dance, in honour of our arrival, followed by a magnificent display of fireworks. We left our sick here and proceeded through a fine country covered with cotton plantations. We were daily in expectation of meeting with the enemy, but they fell back as we advanced in order to gain reinforcements.

On our arrival at the Kishna, a wide and rapid river, we encamped on its banks for a few days to give time for the Madras army under the command of Major-General Sir Thomas Walsh to form a junction with us on the opposite side, where the enemy were said to be in full force, and desirous of giving us battle.

On the following day a party of our grass cutters was attacked in the vicinity of the camp, and driven in with the loss of several of their ponies. This little affair put our commander on the *qui vive*, and the necessary precautions were taken to guard against a surprise.

A picket of one hundred men was ordered out, fifty to remain on duty with loaded arms, and positive orders to shoot anyone who could not repeat the countersign.

The dews were heavy, and as it was impossible to provide tents for the whole of the force, numbers had to bivouac in their cloaks, in consequence of which the cholera broke out to an alarming extent, the young recruits who had lately arrived from England being the first to fall victims to it.

The enemy were not long before they discovered this fact, and believing the moment favourable determined on an attack.

It so happened that I was on picket when the affair commenced. Our party consisted of fifty men, thirty-five dismounted cavalry and twenty-five *sepoys*, while the chain of sentries was composed of twenty-four men, and extended along the banks of the river as far as the bridge so as to prevent the enemy crossing at the only place where it was fordable.

The night was pitch dark, and with the exception of the howling of the jackal, everything was still. Towards midnight I fancied I heard a slight noise, in the direction of the bridge, and mentioned it to the next sentinel, desiring him at the same time to pass the word along. We held ourselves in readiness, and waited some time in breathless attention.

To our rear lay a dense plantation of sugar-cane which flanked the camp and approached almost to the edge of the river, barely leaving space for the line of sentinels to patrol up and down. This afforded ready means of concealment to the enemy, should they succeed in crossing the bridge without notice, and although we felt pretty confident they had not escaped our vigilance we still cast uneasy glances towards it.

After an interval of about ten minutes my notice was again attracted towards the plantation, and listening attentively I heard the foliage distinctly rustling. I challenged, and receiving no answer, fired in the direction from whence the noise proceeded. In an instant about sixty Arabs rushed upon our little party, and a hand to hand fight ensued. The conflict was desperate, and numbers were killed on both sides. Early in the *mêlée* I received a severe cut on the head from a sabre, which laid me senseless on the ground, and would certainly have been despatched, had not a *sepoy* gallantly rushed to my assistance, and by a timely thrust of his bayonet, brought my assailant down. The noise of the firing having reached the inlying picket, they speedily came up, and the enemy took to flight, leaving from twenty to thirty killed and wounded. We had four men killed and several wounded.

An ensign belonging to the *sepoys*, who was on duty with the inlying picket, and who was little more than sixteen years of age, was amongst the first who came up to our assistance. He engaged with a gigantic Arab, and being an expert swordsman, not only baffled every exertion of his huge antagonist to reach him with his knife, but inflicted some severe wounds upon him. Maddened by pain and mortification at being thus baffled by a stripling, the Arab at length threw away his knife, and seizing the blade of his young opponent's sword with his left hand, threw himself upon him, and encircled his slender form with a grasp of iron. The gallant youth struggled ineffectually to free himself, but finding that his assailant was gradually forcing him towards the river in order to cast him into it, he made a last effort, and dragged him in with him. The Arab endeavoured to disengage himself but in vain; despair gave the brave boy strength, and down they both went, firmly locked in each other's embrace.

The failure of this attack dispirited the enemy, and they did not attempt to dispute the passage of the river. Next day we formed a junction with the Madras division, and the enemy fell back on Kolopoor.

We lost no time in advancing towards that place; but as the fortress was built upon a steep rock, and was extremely difficult of approach, we were compelled to halt a few days preparatory to an attack. Negotiations were in the meantime opened by the *rajah*, more, I suspect, with a view of gaining time than of capitulating, as he was daily expecting a large force of Mahratta Horse to come to his aid.

Distrusting the intentions of the enemy, our commander was resolved to be doubly watchful, and the picket duty became extremely severe. A raw youth, from the land of potatoes, who rejoiced in the euphonious patronymic of M'Nulty, was one night placed on sentry at the furthest extremity of the camp, and ordered by the corporal to challenge everyone who approached his post, and in case of his not receiving an answer, to fire.

It so happened that the night was most unfavourable for M'Nulty's first experience of the pleasures of field duty, for the rain descended in torrents, and sentry-boxes not being just then in fashion, poor Paddy was drenched to the skin. His hour of duty having expired, he began to think that the corporal had forgotten him, which was not far from the truth, as the latter was then snoring comfortably in his tent. The sergeant went round with the other relief, but not having been made acquainted with the fact of a sentry being posted where M'Nulty stood, he passed him by, and thus between the two the poor fellow was left another hour on his uncomfortable post.

The unlucky sentry shouted lustily for relief, but the wind was so high, that his voice was borne in every direction but the right one. His vexation at this "dirty turn of the corporal," as he called it, was such, that he debated with himself whether any court martial that had "sinse or raison" could find any man to blame for leaving his post under such a combination of unpleasant circumstances.

Fortunately for him the officer of the picket happened to come by before he had arrived at any satisfactory conclusion. M'Nulty, whose ears were sharp, heard the noise of the distant footsteps, and roared out in a voice of thunder.

"Who goes there?"

"A friend," replied the officer.

"The Lord save us from our friends," replied M'Nulty, in a tone of concentrated bitterness, "it's a quare way you have of shewin' your regard, Mr. Corporal. Has your mother any more of such tendher hearted chickens; if she has, faith it's myself 'ud like to wring the necks off the whole of them, just to privint them tormenting themselves with the misery of their fellow craytures."

"My good fellow," commenced the officer, convulsed with laughter.

"Ah, thin, is it laughin' you are, you crooked nosed son of a ———. Wait till you take me off my post, an' if I don't make you laugh at the wrong side of your face, may I never see sweet Tipperary agin."

"What is the matter, my honest fellow?" said the officer, approaching him, so as that the sentry could now clearly distinguish his rank.

"May I be blessed if I didn't take your honour for the corporal. He has left me here two hours by the clock, an' I haven't a dry rag left on me. Between the rain an' the mud, one might as well be shwimmin' in the bog of Allen."

"You shall be immediately relieved, and I'll punish the lazy rascal for his gross neglect of duty."

"Thank your honour; an' I'll take an airly opportunity myself of letting him into the saycret of my own notions on the subject. I advise him to keep out of my way, or it'll be worse for him, the spalpeen."

"I have a bit of advice to offer you my good fellow, and that is to keep your notions to yourself, for the corporal is your superior, and the articles of war do not altogether approve of such confidential communications as you are disposed to make to him. It is my business to see that his conduct shall not go unpunished."

"Your honour has raison," replied the sentinel, "such low varmint as that isn't worthy of a thrashing."

It is hardly necessary to add that the corporal was reduced, and that M'Nulty was relieved from one embarrassment only to encounter another in the raillery of his comrades.

After remaining idle nearly three weeks, it was at length determined to commence operations. Two companies of the 20th Regiment of Foot as stormers, one wing of the Queen's Royals, two regiments of native infantry, and one company of Foot artillery moved down towards the fort, and took up a commanding position. The cavalry were stationed at the rear of the fort so as to prevent the escape of the *rajah* or any of his family.

The enemy were fully prepared for us, and gave us a hearty welcome, for the fortress mounted some thirty guns of good size and calibre which were well manned. The neighbouring rocks and declivities were held by a numerous body of armed men, who kept up a constant fire from their matchlocks. We opened upon the fort, and our infantry were about to move down, when the enemy unexpectedly ceased firing, and a *faquir* was observed issuing from the fort with a flag of truce. He requested an interview with our commander, which was immediately granted, and after a short conference, he not only acceded unconditionally on the part of the *rajah* to the terms demanded, but agreed to pay the whole of the expenses of the war.

Little or no damage had been done by the firing on either side. The only casualty we had to record, was the loss of Lieutenant Davis of the 4th Madras Native Infantry and four of his men. The deceased officer had command of a small picket, whose duty it was to patrol the lines, so as to prevent the enemy's stragglers from burning or plundering the tents. During the attack on the fort they came across a small body of Arabs, who were going to the relief of the Rajah, but who finding how matters stood were making the beat of their way back. The foremost of the party was challenged, and not answering, Lieutenant Davis attempted to make him prisoner. The man fled, and Lieutenant Davis pursued him, but stumbling into a *nullah* in the chase, the Arab turned upon him and buried his *crease* in his side before any of his men could come to his assistance.

The remainder of the lieutenant's little party maintained an unequal contest with the enemy for some time, and would soon have been overpowered had not a party of cavalry, attracted by the firing, galloped up to their assistance. The Arabs fled in all directions, leaving a number of killed and wounded.

Thus finished the Kolopoor campaign. Our duties were now entirely confined to patrolling the camp, a precaution rendered necessary by the numbers of disbanded mercenaries discharged from the *rajah's* service, who were prowling about the country, killing and plundering every one they met. Finding this a precarious as well as dangerous mode of existence they at length emigrated to a more distant part of Hindostan, and the district was restored to a comparative state of tranquillity.

As positive orders were issued that no European or native soldier should enter the fortress of Kolopoor, I am unable to give my readers a description of the place.

An extensive *bazaar* was formed at a short distance from camp, and the merchants came from the fortress to offer their goods for sale there. They were not a little surprised at the cheerful manner in which we paid our money for everything. Amongst the number of traders who flocked to the place were several *shroffs* or native bankers, who were daily to be seen sitting in their stalls, surrounded by piles of gold *pagodas* and boxes containing costly jewels and ornaments, deposited with them as security for sums advanced on loan.

These temptations proved too strong for the honesty of some of our men. Two of the Madras Native Infantry laid a plan to rob one of the bankers, which was attended with success, owing to the ingenuity with which it was devised.

Towards dusk one of them went to a *shroff*, and having obtained change of some coins pretended he was cheated, in order to occupy the attention of the *choprasses* or native policemen.

During the temporary confusion which ensued, his companion, who had disguised himself as a native, and blackened his face and hands, passed over to a *shroff* at the opposite side, and throwing the contents of a snuff box in his eyes completely blinded him, and made off with a case containing jewels to a large amount.

The *shroff* having recovered from his surprise, roared out "*chure! chure!*" and the uproar became general. The *choprasses* gave chase, but the darkness of the night favoured the thief, and he succeeded in baffling his pursuers for some time.

Becoming exhausted with fatigue, and hearing voices near him, he plunged into a deep *nullah*, but lights were soon moving along its banks, and he saw that his retreat could not long remain undiscovered. Knowing well that whether he restored the property or not, he would be severely punished, he resolved to secure it while there was yet time, and with his bayonet dug a deep hole, in which he buried the casket. Restoring the surface to the same state in which he found it; he twisted the bushes so as to mark the spot, and creeping along on his hands and knees emerged from the *nullah*, and again took to his heels in the direction of the camp.

As ill luck would have it he stumbled on a corporal, and party sent in pursuit of him, and was immediately seized and brought prisoner into camp. His companion had been taken into custody by the *choprasses*.

The two men were tried by a court martial, and sentenced to seven hundred lashes each; and they received their punishment in presence of the assembled brigade. The colonel, who was an exceedingly humane man, entreated of them to disclose where the box was hid, and promised a remission of a portion of their sentence if they would do so; but the fellow who had buried it remained firm, and received his full complement without wincing. The other became insensible before he had received half the number, and was released by order of the colonel.

This ill gotten wealth did not much benefit the thieves: they sold it, and sent the greater portion of the money out of the country for greater security, but the acquisition of so large a sum turned their heads, and they abandoned themselves to every sort of excess. One of them died of fever brought on by drink; and the other purchased his discharge and returned to England. He opened an inn somewhere in Cambridgeshire, but neglecting his business his affairs went to wreck, and he ended his days in the work house.

Chapter 12

An Assassination

Jamais, non jamais de grâce,
Pour l'insolent que l'on va châtier,
Nous allons voir punir l'audace,
De ce coquin de braconnier.

Previous to our departure for Kirkee an assassination was committed on the person of one of our officers, which, owing to the circumstances that provoked it, was very differently viewed by the Europeans and native followers.

As I have already mentioned, the disbanded troops of the *rajah* had formed themselves into bands of plunderers, and scarcely a night passed, without cattle or other property being stolen from the encampment. The apparent impossibility of their penetrating our lines without being detected by the sentries, for some time prevented suspicion from falling in the right quarter, and milch goat after milch goat was nightly carried off, in spite of the efforts made to guard against these depredations.

In order the more effectually to secure them from the thieves, the goats were placed in the *routy*, a small tent appropriated to the use of the native servants, who had strict orders to fire upon, or arrest anyone seen prowling about the tent after nightfall.

One would have supposed that precautions like these would have completely put an end to the thefts, but such was not the case. The goats were missing in even greater numbers than before, and the only way in which these daring robberies could be accounted for was, by collusion between the native servants and the thieves.

An officer named Murray, who had lost several of these useful animals, at length became so annoyed at it, that he determined to keep watch himself for a few nights, in the hope of detecting the plunderers. During his vigils, of course none of his goats disappeared from his *routy*, nor did anything occur to fix his suspicions upon any one. The lieutenant got tired, gave up the watch, and the moment that he did so, the old system was renewed.

The servants to whom the care of the *routy* was entrusted consisted of an old Mussulman, named Ramar, who performed the duties of butler, *a ghorra-walla*, or native horsekeeper, named Goom Singh, and a dressing-boy, aged sixteen, the son of the latter. All three bore irreproachable characters.

The lieutenant rose one morning in no very amiable humour. To say the truth he was not the best tempered man in the world.

"Here Ramar," he shouted, "send Sere Singh to me directly. I am going out shooting."

"*Sahib*," replied Ramar, "*Dooser buckra bogjow*" (another goat is stolen.)

"D——n the *buckra* and you too," exclaimed the impatient lieutenant, "send Sere Singh to me."

"Sere Singh," called out Ramar in his turn. "*Mut jildee, Sahib muntur*" (make haste, master wants you.)

The dressing boy was nowhere to be found. The officer's suspicions were aroused, and he ordered Groom Singh, the father, into his presence.

"That young *looty walla* (thief in grain) of yours has made off with the *buckra*, and mark my words well, *sirrah*, if I do not find him here on my return from shooting, I'll give him *cherry merry bamboo*" (a severe beating with a stick.)

The *ghorra-walla salaamed* his master, but made no reply, well knowing that any attempt at remonstrance would only render him still more violent.

The lieutenant returned about eight o'clock, and having been unsuccessful in his expedition, his ill humour was but too glad to find somebody to vent itself upon.

"Ramar, you d——d black scoundrel," said he to his butler, "have you found the goat?"

"No, *Sahib* me no see *buckra*."

"Talk English, sir, or I'll cut you in two," exclaimed the lieutenant, raising his whip over the shrinking form of the domestic.

"Ah *Sahib*," replied the poor devil, "who take away goat *no mallum*, (I don't understand) the devil come for him, for no *adama puckar*, (nobody could have taken him away)."

"And the boy Sere Singh."

"Here, *sahib*," exclaimed the lad, coming forward.

"Where were you this morning when I called you?" inquired the lieutenant.

"I went to look after the goat, *sahib*."

"More likely to sell it, you young *chure*. Take him to the guard tent, Ramar, and tomorrow I'll have him well flogged."

The boy hearing this, began to cry, and begged to be let off. It was no use, however, he was consigned to the guard tent, and next morning was brought before his master.

"Tell me where you were yesterday when I called you," said the lieutenant, addressing the trembling lad, "and prove that your statement is true."

The boy held down his head, and did not reply.

"Do you hear, sir, if you do not answer me this instant, I'll flog you to the backbone."

"*Hum, mallum ney, sahib , am ney deco, am no puckar*, (I don't understand you, sir; I know nothing about it; I did not steal it.)

"You lying scoundrel I'll flog the truth out of you. What have *you* to say, Goom," he added turning to the father.

The latter addressed the boy in Hindostanee and called on him to swear to the truth of what he had stated. The lad unhesitatingly took the prescribed oath.

"I believe him innocent, *Sahib*," replied the father.

"The devil you do," said the incensed lieutenant. "I have no doubt you know something of the matter yourself. I have a great mind to flog you both, and then I may get at the truth."

"*Marr bok marr, Sahib*," replied the old man, "*um munter, um chokera no marr chokera na mallum*. (Flog away, Sir, I'll bear it patiently, but don't beat my poor boy, he knows nothing about it.)

At the same time he flung off his garments, and desired the *choprassee*, or native policeman, to lay on.

"Seize the youngster," cried the lieutenant, "and give it to him 'till I tell you to stop."

Four stout *ghorra-wallas* laid hold of the lad, and each seizing a limb held him suspended in the air, with his face towards the ground, while the *choprassee* began beating him with a stout bamboo.

The old butler threw himself at the feet of his master, and with tears in his eyes implored of him not to commit such an injustice, for he was satisfied the boy was guiltless of the charge.

"It's no use," said the lieutenant, "I've been robbed by someone, and I'll flog you all round till I find the thief," a threat which he was likely enough to put in execution.

The boy bore his punishment without even a sob escaping him. As soon as he was let loose his father called him over to him.

"Come here, my child," said the old man embracing him. "They have disgraced you for life. Let us quit this accursed spot."

"You will do so at your peril," exclaimed the lieutenant. "If you attempt to stir one step from the encampment I will have you both flogged until there is not a morsel of flesh left upon your backs."

The old man made no reply, but bowed in apparent submission. That same night, however, he and his son made their escape. It was said they had fled to Guzzerat,

About a week after the lieutenant was returning from the mess of the Madras Native Infantry, accompanied by his head servant, when, as he was crossing a field between the two lines, he fancied he was dogged by someone. "Bring the light here, Kamar," he shouted to his attendant, who preceded him at a short distance with a lanthorn. "There is some fellow skulking after us."

The attendant turned quickly, and as he did so, heard a heavy fall and a groan. On running to the spot, he saw his master prostrate on the ground, while Goom Singh stood over him with a brandished knife.

The butler became so terrified that he could make no effort to seize the assassin. The latter cried exultingly, "My boy is revenged," and fled.

Ramar ran for assistance, and returned in a few minutes with the infantry picket. The unfortunate officer was conveyed to his quarters, where he breathed his last shortly after his arrival.

Every exertion was made by the authorities to bring the murderer to justice. Large rewards were offered for his apprehension, and tempting promises held out to the son, who was discovered lurking in the neighbourhood, but all their efforts were fruitless, he was never after heard of.

Everything being now arranged for our departure, we left Kolopoor in March, and arrived at Kirkee shortly before the setting in of the monsoon.

Here we found a new colonel, who had just arrived from England. He had the reputation of being a terrible martinet, and the first opportunity he had of addressing the regiment, did not diminish the unpleasant impression which such a character is calculated to make on those placed under his command.

The morning after our arrival he ordered a foot parade, and the regiment having been formed into a square, he rode into the centre and addressed us in the following characteristic style.

> Non commissioned officers and men, I have a few words to say to you—they shall be brief, but take care and pay attention to them. I have been honoured by His Majesty with a commission in this regiment; and as I am determined to do *my* duty, you will save me and yourselves a great deal of trouble by doing yours. Come before me as seldom as you can, for whenever you do, you'll find you have no lamb to play with.

Our commander had closed this short but significant harangue when the adjutant stepped forward and whispered something in his ear. The colonel immediately called out:

> Men, I quite forgot to tell you that Government has been pleased to build nine pretty little cottages (*congee* houses) for your use. It will do you no harm to take a look at them in the course of the day; but for my part I must candidly tell you, I don't much like these new fashioned contrivances; there is nothing like getting your full allowance, and having done with it at once.

In consequence of the decrease in our numbers, occasioned by the cholera and Guzzerat fever, it became necessary to obtain volunteers, wherever they could be procured. Unfortunately for us His Majesty's 41st regiment of Foot happened at this time to be on the eve of its departure for England, and about forty men volunteered from that corps. It was the first and only instance of the kind that fell under my observation and the result of the experiment was not a happy one. With one or two exceptions, the whole of the new draft turned out bad and inefficient dragoons, whether from the inconsistency of the habits of the two services or individual incapacity, I cannot take upon myself to say. In vain the riding master endeavoured to initiate them in the mysteries of horsemanship; they daily met with severe accidents at field exercise, which laid them up in hospital, and rendered them unfit for duty.

A representation of the fact having been made to the authorities, they abandoned any further attempt to reconcile habits so entirely at variance with each other.

Amongst the new volunteers that joined us was a desperate character, named Madill, whose fame had preceded him from his former regiment, and whose exploits amongst us proved that his evil qualities had not been exaggerated. Like most reprobates who embrace a military life, as the last resort of a profligate and abandoned career, this man had received a good education, which served only to place his vices in a more detestable light.

So great was the horror entertained of him in his own regiment, that when it became known he wished to volunteer into the dragoons, the quartermaster who had previously served with us, and who had a strong regard for his old corps, endeavoured to dissuade him from his purpose, offering even to furnish him with a complete kit, if he would confer the benefit of his services on one of the infantry regiments in Madras or Bengal.

"It's no use, sir," replied Madill, "I've been handling brown Bess and Pompey long enough, and I'll now ride and dragoon it a bit for my own pleasure."

He had not long joined us at Kirkee, when he discovered that in abandoning Brown Bess and Pompey for the dragooning life, he had not made an exchange for the better. The difficulty of acquiring the necessary qualifications for a dragoon, at all times great, seemed to him insuperable. He either could not, or would not accustom himself to the stable duties. Punishment necessarily followed neglect, and then all the evil qualities of the man became again aroused.

Being a muscular and powerfully built man, he never lost an opportunity of bullying or oppressing those who were weaker than himself. Ferocious and vindictive, in character, he resorted to treachery where he knew open force could not be employed with safety. Such a happy junction of qualities could not fail to render him at once a bad soldier and a worse comrade.

To such an extent was this ruffian dreaded, that it was with evident reluctance the men obeyed the order to convey him to the guard-house whenever he misconducted himself. It was a service of danger, for he did not scruple to employ his teeth where he was deprived of other means of resistance.

In one of his drunken fits he was sent as usual to the guard-house, where he found himself face to face with a sergeant for whom he had conceived an inveterate hatred, and whose life he had frequently threatened.

Madill was in one of those rabid humours in which it became dangerous to approach him. He no sooner saw the sergeant than he commenced loading him with the most opprobrious epithets, and exhibited a disposition to assault him. The sergeant told him to be quiet, or he would place him in confinement in the *congee* houses.

"Will you, by G——," exclaimed Madill, snatching a sword from the wall. "Then I'll give you something to make you remember me before I go."

Making a lunge at the sergeant, he would have run him through the body, had not the latter evaded the thrust, by slipping aside. The guard instantly rushed upon him, and secured him with handcuffs after a desperate resistance, in which his teeth were, as usual, employed upon his assailants. It now became advisable, for the safety of all, that he should be removed to a place of confinement, where he would have no opportunity of exercising his cannibal propensities, and the assistance of some of the native followers having been called in, he was carried, or rather dragged, to the *congee* houses.

It unfortunately so happened that at this period none of the cells were tenantless, and it became necessary to place him in company with another culprit. Someone suggested that it would be better to put three of the other prisoners together; but this could not be done, as there was a strict order against more than two being confined in the same cell.

The cell selected was already occupied by a dragoon named Devine, who belonged to the same troop as Madill, and was known to be at enmity with him. How this circumstance should have been overlooked by the non commissioned officer surprises me, as frequent fights had occurred between the parties, and their hostility was notorious to everyone.

I have heard Devine subsequently declare, that he never, in his life, entertained a sensation of fear, until he saw the door of his cell opened to admit this ferocious ruffian. In his first alarm, he attempted to rush out, but was instantly struck back by the guard, who, having by time unbound Madill, (not a little stupefied by the force which had been employed to convey him to his cell) by a simultaneous and vigorous push, drove him headlong into his prison. The double doors were instantly secured, and Devine lay crouched in a corner watching the movements of his enemy.

Madill lay for some time perfectly quiet, and appeared to have fallen into a profound slumber. His companion began to hope that his strength had been exhausted in the struggle, and that he would feel no disposition to molest him, for he well knew that unless such were the case, there was but little chance of his escaping his fangs. He also comforted himself with the reflection that as the cell was extremely dark, there was a possibility of his not recognising him; but he did not know his man, for it mattered little to Madill on whom he vented his rage.

At the expiration of about a quarter of an hour he awoke and shook himself with a growl not unlike that of a tiger. Hearing the breathing of another in the cell, he demanded with an execration who it was? Devine feigned sleep, but that would not do; Madill started up, and shaking him roughly, again enquired who he was.

The poor fellow disguised his voice as well as he was able, in the hope of deceiving him, but being an Irishman, the ruse did not succeed, and a roar of savage exultation announced he was detected. He bounded instantly to his feet, and prepared for a contest which he felt was inevitable. The other sprang upon him, and seizing him by the throat, held him at arm's length for several minutes.

"So you thought I didn't know you, Devine," exclaimed the ruffian. "Know you. Indeed! I'd smell an enemy in the dark, and I'll have your blood now, if I am to swing for it."

"You surely do not mean to murder me?" replied the other. "What have I done to you?"

"I'll tell you what you have done, you chicken-hearted spy. You told the sergeant of the room that I hadn't been in bed the night the canteen was broken open, and since then they've kept a close eye on me. Your pimping and tale-bearing have brought me into disgrace, and I'll teach you what it is to meddle with other men's affairs."

Devine was a strong, active young fellow, though inferior in physical power to the other. Despair, however, lent him strength, and convinced that his assailant would take his life, he resolved to sell it as dearly as he could.

The struggle that ensued was a desperate one. The two men became locked together, and rolled about the floor gnashing their teeth with rage, and endeavouring to throttle each other. At length Madill began to use his teeth, and bit large pieces out of the flesh of his opponent. The latter cried aloud for help, in his agony.

The sentry on duty hearing the noise, passed the alarm to the sergeant of the guard; but the latter did not make his appearance for upwards of a quarter of an hour. During this time the cries of the unfortunate Devine were becoming fainter and fainter, and at length wholly ceased.

On the doors being opened, the scene that presented itself was truly shocking. In a corner of the cell lay Devine apparently dead, his features hardly retaining a vestige of humanity, so lacerated were they by the numerous wounds inflicted by the teeth of his murderous assailant. The latter lay stretched across his body in almost as helpless a state, but in reality more exhausted than injured.

Devine was removed to hospital in a state of insensibility. The injuries he had received proved of so serious a nature that he was incapacitated for further service, and was ultimately discharged.

Madill was brought before a court martial, and sentenced to severe corporal punishment. This, however, had no effect in correcting the ferocity of his character, and he was at length sentenced to a long term of solitary confinement. His constitution, impaired by excess, soon gave way, under this punishment, and he was removed from prison only to finish his career in the hospital.

Chapter 13

A Duel

I will show you, slaves,
How you should be commanded, and who led you.

In order to form the regiment after the accession of so many inexperienced volunteers, it became necessary to have daily field drills, so as to be in a state of tolerable preparation for the ensuing half yearly inspection.

The officers, on first joining, are also subjected to frequent drilling, more particularly in that branch called field exercise. The sooner the officer makes himself thoroughly acquainted with his duties, the more agreeable he will find his position, as it must be anything but pleasant for patrician blood to find itself under the orders of a sergeant major.

One field day, it so happened that a young cornet who had lately exchanged from the infantry, found himself placed under the command of a sergeant major, named Donovan, who, though a good disciplinarian, was unfortunately addicted to intemperate habits, and on this particular occasion, was not entirely recovered from the effects of his previous night's libations.

On the formation of the squadrons Cornet, G——, the officer in question, had the command of the right troop, another subaltern that of the left, while the sergeant major commanded the squadron from the centre.

The squadron having been properly told off, proceeded with the others to the drill ground. I should mention that our new cornet was a consummate fop, and, like all young officers, impatient of the least reply on the part of the men, whom he was in the habit of committing to the guard room for the most trifling and imaginary offences. These facts rendered the scene I am about to describe highly amusing.

As the troop was manoeuvring, under the orders of the colonel, who was exceedingly rapid in all his movements, the sergeant major discovered that Cornet G—— was utterly incapable of managing his men.

"Troops, right wheel, forward," shouted the sergeant major in quick succession, as we broke into column, preparing to counter-march upon our centre.

The cornet got bewildered, took up the word of command as "left wheel," and gave it accordingly. The troop wheeled to the reverse hand, when the sergeant major finding everything thrown into confusion, thundered out, "Threes right, right wheel, front form."

This brought the troop again into its proper place; and the sergeant major, turning round to the cornet, angrily addressed him,

"What the devil are you about, sir? Another mistake, after all the pains I have taken with you," and then turning half aside, he muttered audibly, "May I be d——d if he isn't as stupid as an ass."

The officer bit his lips with vexation, but had the good sense not to make any reply. The men enjoyed his humiliation, and a general titter ran through the troop.

"Into line," was the next order. This brought us into our proper position.

"By the flank, march off threes; right thrown back," again shouted the colonel.

"Threes right," repeated the sergeant major, and off we proceeded at a canter to our new alignment.

By another unfortunate mischance the cornet got placed in a wrong position. Instead of being in front of his troop he found himself at the rear.

"Here, Sir," roared the sergeant major, enraged beyond all power of self-control. "You must be infernally stupid to make such a blunder as that. If you go on in that way you will bring me and my squadron into disgrace with the colonel."

This proved too much for the cornet, who, perceiving that the men were grinning at him, angrily replied:

"You are drunk, and I'll report you to the colonel for your impertinence."

"Front," shouted the colonel, "the line will attack."

"Perhaps, Sir," said the sergeant major addressing the cornet in a jeering tone, "you'd like to take up the squadron."

The cornet believing him serious, replied instantly.

"I shall do so. Change places,"

As the sergeant major anticipated, the cornet was not a sufficiently good horseman to keep up the advance. The consequence was that as soon as the charge sounded he found himself hustled about in the centre of the squadron by the men, who owed him no good will, and ultimately in the rear, just where he ought not to be.

The halt now sounded, and the sergeant major was of course obliged to resume his place in order to restore something like order."

The cornet had by this time made his way to the front foaming with rage.

"I'll have every man of you sent to drill," he exclaimed, "how dare you ride over me? You are all leagued against me by that rascally sergeant-major."

The latter who had been chuckling at the mortification of the young officer, now addressed him in rather a peremptory tone.

"Be good enough to go to the rear, sir. Here sergeant," he added, turning to another non-commissioned officer, "take the troop."

The cornet, unable to control his anger, rode directly to the colonel. The latter was then too much occupied to attend to him, and directed him to wait till the field day was over.

At the conclusion of the drill, he heard the cornet's complaint, and sent the adjutant to report if the sergeant major was drunk as had been represented to him. The latter reported in the affirmative, and Donovan was immediately placed under arrest. He was brought to a court martial, and reduced to the rank and pay of a private. Owing to his abilities as a drill, he was however shortly after restored to the rank of sergeant.

Of the cornet I have only to add that he never made a good cavalry officer. He has since exercised a sound discretion in again exchanging into an infantry regiment.

Having just at this period attained the rank of sergeant I found myself as it were transferred to a new station in society, and appreciating the comforts and enjoyments it afforded me, I determined to keep it if I could by my good behaviour. I had long experienced the want of some other resource than the canteen for the occupation of my leisure hours, and finding a disposition on the part of the other sergeants to second my efforts, I determined on forming a library for the non commissioned officers, and accordingly made an application to the colonel for leave to write to London for books.

The old martinet stared at me as if he did not exactly comprehend me.

"A what," said he.

"A library, sir—a non-commissioned officer's library."

"A library, and what the devil do you want with a library? No, no, you want to make the men all lawyers, and we have too many of them already. If things go on like this, you'll soon take the command of the regiment out of my hands. The only two books fit for a soldier, are the articles of war and the bible."

"Then, sir, since you'll not allow us to have books, perhaps you'll give us leave to subscribe for a few newspapers."

"To teach you sedition, and make you more rebellious than you are. May I ask which are the newspapers and the politics to which you pin your faith, sergeant?"

I felt the sarcastic tone in which this was uttered, but dare not of course make any reply, further than to state that we wished to have the *Atlas, Sunday Times,* and *Weekly Despatch.*

The colonel bounded from his chair as if struck by a bullet on hearing the name of the latter paper, which about this time contained a series of excellent articles on corporal punishment.

"How dare you propose such a thing?" he exclaimed in one of those bursts of anger which rendered him unsafe to approach. "Admit a lying, seditious publication like that amongst His Majesty's troops— I'd sooner cut off my right arm first, and I've a great mind to put you under arrest for your impertinence in even naming it."

"Why, sir, the *Despatch* is already received in the regiment by some of the men."

"That is no reason why I should allow the evil to spread further. Once for all I tell you that I am not one of your 'march of intelligence' men. I never knew a good soldier yet who was fond of your trashy books or seditious newspapers, and I shall not be the first to introduce such a bad precedent into the service."

Against such arguments as these, there was of course, no use in reasoning, and I left the colonel's presence completely crest fallen, and determined not to take any further step in the matter until another change took place in the command of the regiment, an event which I had not long to wait for, owing to the climate, and a splenetic temperament rendering a return to England an alternative of life or death with our anti "march of intelligence" commander.

Our new colonel was a man of enlarged views and cultivated mind, and so far from raising objections to my plan gave it his ready patronage and assistance, and in a short time we laid the foundation of an excellent library both for non-commissioned officers and men. To show the success which attended the experiment, I have only to mention that the twenty-five pounds a quarter subscriptions, with which we commenced, had risen to one hundred by the time we left India.

I do not know anything more calculated to reform dissipated habits, or prevent the young soldier from degenerating into them than resources of this kind. There are many men in the army who have really no taste for the drunken and noisy atmosphere of the pot-house, who are driven to it by the absence of mental occupation. Once there the effects of drink, or the force of example, betrays them into other excesses, and degradation and punishment follow as a matter of course.

In May, 1827, the officers of one of His Majesty's regiments stationed at Poona determined on giving a ball and supper on a large scale, so as to include the civilians and their wives as well as the whole of the officers of the brigade. Extensive preparations were accordingly made—a large marquee was added to the already spacious mess room of the regiment—bricklayers were set to work to pull down and reconstruct, and the services of everyone who had the least talent for decoration were put in requisition.

The evening fixed for this long talked of *fête* arrived, and the appearance which the rooms presented was pretty enough.

An arcade formed of evergreens and temporarily floored and covered with matting formed the entrance to the suite, and being tastefully lit up with variegated lamps had an extremely gay effect. The ball room was decorated with the colours of the regiment, the memorials of their Peninsular exploits, and the royal aim? with the motto "*welcome all*" crowned the whole.

Amongst the officers of our regiment present was Lieutenant G——, one of the finest men in the army, but a noted duellist. He had only just arrived from Bengal, where he had fought a lieutenant colonel commanding a regiment of Native Infantry, and severely wounded him.

A waltz having been struck up by the band, Lieut. G——, who excelled in this accomplishment, led out Mrs. W——, the wife of an old captain of the Madras Native Infantry, who was then playing piquet in the card room. The lady was young, beautiful, and graceful, and the waltzing of this highly gifted couple attracted universal attention.

As soon as supper was announced, Captain W—— rejoined his lady, but returned again to the card table as soon as the dancing was resumed,

When he had concluded his game he sought his wife for the purpose of taking her home, as it was now late, and they had a considerable distance to go. The lady was, however, nowhere to be found, and by a suspicious coincidence Lieut. G—— was also missing.

To render the case still stronger against the latter, one of the native servants stated that he had seen an officer put Mrs. W—— into a *palankeen* about an hour before.

The captain became furious at this intelligence, and happening to meet a brother officer and particular friend of Lieut. G—— at the entrance to the ballroom as he was prosecuting his enquiries, he said to him in a tone of voice which could be heard by all the servants in the passage.

"You are a friend of Lieut. G——, Sir?"

"I have that honour, Captain W——."

"Then you are the friend of one of the greatest scoundrels that ever breathed."

"You had better reserve those expressions for Lieut. G—— himself, captain."

"I would if I knew where to find him. In the meantime you will do me a favour by communicating them to him."

"Oh, as for that matter he will soon be here," replied the other. "William, go to the billiard room, and tell Lieut. G—— that he is wanted here directly."

"If he is in the billiard room," said Captain W——," you need not send your servant. The more public the opportunity of exposing him the better I shall at once go there."

"You will please to recollect, Captain W——," said the other, "that I have the first claim upon you, as you have grossly insulted me by connecting me with the atrocious language you have just uttered."

"I will meet you, sir, but Lieut. G—— is first on my list. If you like to follow me, you will have the gratification of hearing me repeat to your friend what I have just said to you."

Striding towards the billiard room, he entered it just as Lieut. G—— was on the point of making a stroke.

"What have you done with my wife, Sir?" cried Captain W—— as he rushed up the room. "Answer me without equivocation or I'll brain you on the spot!"

Lieut. G—— arrested the movement of his queue, and looking towards the captain replied with imperturbable coolness, "I shall be at your service presently," and next minute holed his adversary's ball.

"Seven, five," he continued addressing the marker, then turning to Captain W—— who became still more enraged at the impassability of his manner, he said, "you did me the favour of addressing me just now."

"I did. Sir. I desire to know what you have done with my wife?"

"Upon my honour, Captain W——, I know nothing whatever of the lady."

"Liar and villain!" exclaimed the husband. "Take that to teach you what it is to trifle with the feelings of others," and raising his clenched hand he struck him full in the face.

The lieutenant staggered under the force of the blow, but recovering himself in a moment said, in the same unmoved tone of voice,

"I need not tell you, Captain W——. that the outrage you have just committed on me is one that must be promptly satisfied."

"The sooner the better, sir," replied the other.

"I have only to send for my pistols to Kirkee and I shall be ready. In the meantime you had better get a friend, and you will find me in the Wood Yard in an hour from this."

"I shall be there to the moment."

Lieut. G—— immediately left the room, and chancing to meet me in the passage called me aside, and told me to saddle his pony and gallop to his quarters for a small mahogany case which was to be found in his drawers.

I knew nothing of what had occurred, and of course obeyed his orders without a moment's hesitation. I reached Kirkee in about half of an hour, and having obtained what I was sent for, returned to Poona in about the same time.

On re-entering the billiard room I found Lieut. G—— quietly pursuing his game. The moment he saw me he quitted it, and took the ease from me, after thanking me for the haste I had made,

I turned into the *lazarette*, or refreshment room, and there I saw Captain W—— folding up and sealing some letters. As soon as he had done he looked at his watch, and quitted the room. I had not been more than from fifteen to twenty minutes in the *lazarette* when the report of firearms was distinctly heard above the music of the band, and the hum of voices in the ball room.

Half suspecting from the errand on which I had been sent that something was wrong, I ran out in the direction of the Wood Yard, from whence the reports proceeded.

Several others, who were either aware of what had occurred or who had been attracted like myself by the noise, were to be seen hurrying towards the same spot.

The Wood Yard was a large quadrangle formed by logs of wood, and was about fifty feet square and twenty high, with an entrance at the south side. On gaining the interior a melancholy scene presented itself.

By the light of a couple of torches borne by native servants, and throwing a strong glare on the faces of the group, several officers were to be seen stooping over the body of a wounded man, whose features were already convulsed by the agonies of death. At a little distance stood Lieut. G——, and practised duellist as he was he seemed as terror stricken as the most guilty murderer. His face was ghastly pale, and his whole frame trembled with agitation. Two of his friends were endeavouring to hurry him from the spot; but he paid no attention to their entreaties, so completely was his mind engrossed by the terrible spectacle before him. Finding persuasion useless, they were eventually obliged to drag him away by force.

The news had by this time reached the ball room, and threw the gay scene into confusion. The near presence of death is at all times a subject for grave reflection, but the lesson is doubly impressive when it comes to us in the midst of enjoyment.

The body of Captain W—— was conveyed to his quarters, and a court of enquiry held upon it. His unhappy opponent made his escape, but soon after surrendered and took his trial. He was honourably acquitted, it having been shown that he had received the most unmerited provocation, Mrs. W—— having in fact eloped with another officer, who had long been paying her attention.

Chapter 14

Sergeant Morgan

That I have ta'en away this old man's daughter,
It is most true; true I have married her;
The very head and front of my offending
Hath this extent no more.

The cavalry regiments in India are, for the most part, supplied with horses by the Arab or Persian dealers, who visit the presidencies twice or thrice a-year.

In 1833, I was sent to Pamwell with a sergeant named Morgan, to meet one of these horse dealers, and bring back about fifty head of cattle, which had been passed by the committee of inspection at Bombay. We were accompanied by a numerous body of *grhorra-wallas*.

On reaching our destination, we found Abdallah Khorassan, the well known Persian dealer awaiting our arrival. He had pitched his tent under the shade of a large tamarind tree, near which stood a *hackery*, which served both as the travelling equipage and sleeping place of his daughter.

Report spoke highly of the beauty of this maiden, and the occasional glimpses we caught of her graceful figure and tiny feet, encased in slippers of green and gold, increased the desire we felt to behold her features. The jealous watchfulness of the father, who had only been prevailed on to allow her to accompany him on this expedition, by the pressing entreaties of some of her mother's relations at Surat, who were anxious to see her, and the as wakeful vigilance of the driver of the *hackery*, who was an old and attached servant of Abdallah combined, however, for some time to defeat our wishes.

We were obliged to remain at Pamwell about a week, in order to await the orders of the commissariat, and during this interval we availed ourselves of every possible opportunity of obtaining a sight of the young Persian. Chance at length favoured my comrade.

I should have mentioned that Morgan was the son of an old soldier who had volunteered from the 17th Light Dragoons into our regiment, and who had passed most of his life in India. This young man was only seven years old when he arrived in the Presidency, and as children are quick in acquiring languages, he was not long in obtaining such a proficiency in Hindostanee, that he spoke it almost like a native. He was a fine, dashing young fellow, about six feet in height, and one of the best horsemen in the regiment.

Amongst the cattle which Abdallah had brought with him, were a beautiful Arabian horse, valued at five hundred pounds, which had been purchased from him by Major Mansfield, who kept a racing stud at Poona, and a cream-coloured pony of the same breed, which was intended for a lady in Bombay, but who left it on his hands on account of the exorbitancy of the price asked for it. This latter was as vicious a little animal as I ever met with, but an especial favourite with its owner, who had it attached to his tent, and never suffered it to be removed from under his own eye.

Having formed a favourable opinion of Morgan's abilities in the management of horses, Abdallah asked him if he would undertake to lunge his pony for him. To this proposition the other joyfully assented, knowing that it would bring him into the immediate neighbourhood of the *hackery*, and perhaps give him an opportunity of conversing with the fair Persian.

This propitious circumstance was not long in producing the desired result, As Morgan exercised the pony, he could detect a pair of bright eyes watching his movements through an aperture in the covering of the vehicle, and by degrees a sort of telegraphic communication was established between them. This, however, did not satisfy the ardent desires of the adventurous sergeant and he eagerly watched an opportunity of having an interview with her.

He had not long to wait. Learning that she usually left the *hackery* before sunrise, to perform her ablutions at a neighbouring stream, he cautiously followed her, and concealing himself behind the trunk of a large banyan tree, awaited a fitting moment to present himself before her. Ignorant of a spectator being so near, she removed her veil, and displayed features which at once riveted the chains of the enamoured sergeant.

On his making his appearance, she screamed with terror, and hastily replaced her veil. Morgan addressed her in soothing tones and assured her that his only motive in following her was to protect her from the tigers who were in the habit of descending to water from the neighbouring mountains.

She thanked him for his kindness, and telling him she would inform her father of it, was about to return to the tents when Morgan threw himself at her feet and seizing her hand poured forth the most extravagant protestations of love, and modestly entreated her to reward his devotion by eloping with him.

The girl became terrified at his earnestness, and fancying he meant to offer her violence swooned away.

The sergeant supported her in his arms, and soon revived her by sprinkling cold water on her face. He could not however help imprinting two or three kisses on her beautiful features whilst the opportunity offered, and it was the half consciousness of this, or the novel sensation of finding herself in the arms of a stranger, that suffused her face and neck with deep blushes as she recovered animation:

"Begone," she faintly uttered, "for if my father finds us thus he will kill you."

"I will not leave you," said Morgan, "until you first promise me that you will turn a favourable ear to my prayers."

"Alas! Christian," she replied, "what would you have of me. The laws of your religion forbid your marrying anyone but a member of your own creed, and your mistress I can never be."

"And what is to prevent your becoming a Christian," said Morgan encouraged by the half yielding tone of this reply, "and thus removing the only obstacle to our happiness."

"Never," cried the girl with sudden energy, as she escaped from his grasp and fled with the fleetness of a fawn towards her father's tents.

Morgan returned full of hope, and communicated to me the particulars of the morning's interview. I saw nothing in them to warrant the sanguine expectations he had formed; but he appeared convinced he should be able to conquer the girl's obstinacy, and told me he had made up his mind to carry her off.

"Have you reflected on the consequences of the step you are about to take?" I asked.

"Yes," he said, "I shall probably lose my rank, but I shall have gained what I prize infinitely more."

We next day received the route for Kirkee, and set out the same evening for Choke, accompanied by Abdallah and his daughter. We reached Capoolee at the foot of the Bhor Ghauts on the following morning, and after resting ourselves for the day prepared to ascend these stupendous heights.

Morgan led the advance with the *ghorra-wallas*, preceded at a short distance by the *hackery*. Abdallah and myself rode together in the rear, and owing to the age of my companion we made but slow progress compared with that of the remainder of the party. Morgan had at least three quarters of an hour's start of us, and he took care to avail himself of it. On arriving at the platform which crowns the summit of the ascent, he managed to send the driver of the *hackery* to a neighbouring village in search of provisions, and thus obtained another opportunity of conversing with the young Persian.

On coming up with him, I asked him to take charge of the lines, and then went with Abdallah as far as the commissariat stores to draw forage for the use of the cattle. The waggons containing the stores were situated at the distance of about a quarter of a mile from the tents for the convenience of water, and we were detained there about half an hour.

On returning to the lines, the horse dealer proceeded straight to his tent, and the evening meal being ready, I sent one of the *ghorra-wallas* to look for Morgan. He was nowhere to be found.

Being rather hungry ad impatient of delay, I sat down, but had not been many minutes at my meal when I saw Abdallah approaching, with an air of extreme alarm.

On reaching me, he demanded if I knew what had become of his daughter.

"How should I know more than yourself?" I replied. "I have not left you since our arrival here."

"Where is Morgan Sahib?" he anxiously inquired, as if a new idea had struck him.

"I know not," I answered. "I have sent several persons to look after him, and he is nowhere to be found."

"Dogs of Christians," said the old man, tearing his hair and rolling himself in the dust. "You have conspired to rob me of my child. Oh that I should ever have been induced to trust her amongst you!"

At this moment the driver of the hackery, who had been to the village to look for provisions, came running up to his master, and informed him he had met Morgan, mounted on his favourite Arabian steed, with his daughter seated behind him. The horse was galloping at such a pace, that it was impossible to arrest their flight, and the fugitives had taken the direction of the village of Wargam.

Nothing could equal the distraction and fury of the bereaved father. He made three several attempts to stab himself, and it was only by force that I could restrain him. As soon as he was restored to something like calmness, he sent the whole of his followers down the *ghauts* after them, naturally concluding they would take shipping at Pamwell, and proceed to Bombay. Instead of that, however, they dashed right across the country, and succeeded in baffling all pursuit.

On arriving at headquarters, I immediately made a report of the circumstance to the adjutant, and the father went to lodge his complaint before the colonel himself.

Early on the following morning, the Arabian, which had been taken, was sent to the barracks, with a note addressed to me, containing a request from Morgan that I would inform Abdallah his daughter was perfectly safe, and that he would make him the only reparation in his power by marrying her.

This only served to exasperate the old man still more. He stormed and raved, and finally quitted the barracks swearing by all his gods he would never see her again.

Every effort was made by the authorities to discover the retreat of the fugitives, but in vain; and it was not till some weeks after that Morgan returned to his duty, accompanied by his young Christian wife, whose beauty became the theme of admiration amongst his comrades, and the envy of their wives.

As the colonel could not overlook so glaring a breach of discipline, he had the sergeant brought before a court martial, and he was sentenced to be reduced and imprisoned for a short term.

Owing to the peculiar circumstances of the case, and his previous irreproachable character, he soon regained his former rank, and his was amongst the few instances of happiness in the married state that have fallen under my observation in the army.

Abdallah continued to visit the cantonments as usual, twice or thrice a-year, but he never could be prevailed on to see his daughter again.

The greatest embarrassment which a young officer experiences on entering a cavalry regiment is in the equitation drill. The better the horseman he may have been in private life, the more difficult it is to break him into the cavalry system. Many a ludicrous proof of this has fallen under my observation.

Being attached to the riding department as drill sergeant, I went one evening to receive my orders from our worthy riding master.

"Let me see! the first ride of young men may have their swords: and let your ride take up stirrups tomorrow. Cornet Sherman will join your ride, for the others can make nothing of him. Try if you can succeed. It is a pity that so fine a young fellow cannot ride."

"I will do my best. Sir," I replied, and withdrew.

Next morning the cornet made his appearance in the riding school and enquired for me.

"This way, Sir," I called out, "please to step into the riding school, and I'll join you in a few minutes."

I then went and selected a horse which I knew would put the cornet's equestrian skill to a severe test. I should mention that the riding school was covered with tan, and that a fall was not likely to be attended with serious consequences.

"A fine horse this, Sir," said I, leading the vicious brute into the riding school, where the cornet stood. "As gentle as a lamb, though full of spirit."

"Beautiful animal indeed, serjeant."

"Been much accustomed to riding, Sir?"

"Since my childhood. I have been living in a famous sporting country, and have been in the habit of going out twice a week with the hounds."

"Oh, then I haven't much to teach you. Sir. You'll find everything come easy to you."

The cornet winced, recollecting his previous failures in the riding school, but said nothing.

The ride of young men having been formed, I called to Mr. Sherman to mount, and to fall in two files from the right.

He had not been many minutes in the saddle when his horse commenced kicking furiously, owing to his being held badly in hand.

The cornet, who I verily believe had never mounted a horse before he joined us, held valiantly with both hands to his holsters, and cried out in great alarm—

"For God sake assist me, sergeant, or I shall be off."

I seized the reins, and helped the frightened officer to descend.

"What is the matter. Sir; you must have mismanaged your horse, for he is one of the gentlest in the regiment."

"Matter! he's been near breaking my neck, the d——d brute. Give me another, for I shall not mount him again."

"Why I thought from what you told me just now, sir, that you would mount anything,"

"Yes, anything but such an incarnate devil as that. He does nothing but kick."

"Well, try this one, sir. Here, Hardy, change horses with this gentleman. A lady might ride him."

The cornet mounted, and having fallen in, I called out:

"Ride! attention! by your right march. Cornet, sit down in your saddle, and keep your body upright. Shoulders well back, if you please."

"Right, turn! Very well. Leading file, circle. Now, men, I'll try a trot; every horse off at the same time. Trot!"

The cornet swung terribly in his saddle, and received bump after bump from his horse, which was a famous trotter, until his nether man must have been pounded into a most woeful condition. He endeavoured to prevent us perceiving what he was suffering, and his countenance betrayed a ludicrous struggle between pain and affected ease.

"Leading file, change. Trot out! Right, turn! Steady, cornet. Shorten your reins, sir."

"Stirrups up!"

"You surely do not mean that, sergeant. I shall never be able to keep my seat if you take my stirrups from me."

"You an old huntsman, and not to be able to ride without stirrups, sir. I never heard of such a thing."

"But it's different riding over a clear country, and amongst a crowd in a confined space like this."

"Come, come sir, you must have your stirrups up, or I shall have them taken away."

Seeing that he had nothing for it but to obey, he reluctantly took them up.

"Left, turn."

The cornet again caught hold of the holsters as this manoeuvre was performed.

As the files came wheeling round, I suddenly shouted out, "Halt," which brought the cornet's horse to a standstill, and his rider plump into the tan.

"No bones broken, I hope, sir"

"It isn't your fault that I haven't, Mr. Serjeant," replied the discomfited officer, as he gathered himself up.

"My fault!" said I, with the most innocent air imaginable. "I cannot see how I am to blame, sir; I have only put you through the ordinary riding-school lesson."

"If that be the case, I'll have no more of your lessons. It was never intended that a man should ride without stirrups."

"Oh, this is only what occurs to everyone commencing the cavalry drill, sir; you must not let it discourage you. Try again, and my life on it, you will succeed better."

"But will you let me have my stirrups?"

"If you will have it so, sir, though it's rather against the rules. That's right, cornet, I see you don't mind a fall. I'll tell you what, men, if I see any more tittering, I'll send some of you to the guard room. Ride! attention! tell off by files from the right! Trot! Form double ride. Right and left, turn."

The cornet's horse not being kept well in hand, flew at the opposite file. In an instant the two animals were on their haunches, and the unfortunate officer lay sprawling again in the dust.

Jumping to his feet, in the fear of being trampled on by the furious animals, his hair and features smothered in tan, the frightened cornet rushed to the door of the riding school; but finding it locked, he cried out to me to let him out.

"I hope you are not really hurt, sir," said I, as I approached the door to comply with his wishes.

"You d——d rascal," he replied, "I'll report you to the riding master, for your conduct. What do you mean by putting me on a furious kicker, and then on a rabid biter like that."

"They are the horses used in the school, sir, and if you are not able to manage them, it is not my fault. If you had not told me you were in the habit of going out to hunt I might probably have mounted you on one of the ladies' ponies."

This was too much for him, so vaulting over the half door of the riding school, he posted straight to the riding-master with his complaint. The latter could not help smiling at the plight in which he appeared.

"What another tumble, cornet," He exclaimed. "This is really too bad, it shows a great falling off in your horsemanship," and the worthy officer chuckled at the pun he had made.

"It is the fault of that d——d scamp you employ then. He picks me out the most vicious brutes in the riding school list, in order to break my neck or have my head bit off. It has been nothing but trot trot all the morning with stirrups up. I have a great mind to go to the colonel and make him a present of my commission, in order to have the satisfaction of thrashing that fellow."

"Take my advice," observed the riding-master, "and say nothing more on the subject You are only experiencing what everyone else has had to go through on entering the cavalry, and if you make any work about it, you will only expose yourself to the jests and ridicule of your brother officers. Come to the riding school in the morning, and we will see if you cannot make better progress than this."

The cornet had good sense enough to take the hint, and having conquered his foolish fears, soon became as good a horseman as any in the service.

The regiment having been now nearly twenty years in India, we looked forward with eagerness to the news of our recall; not so much from discontentment with our position, as from a natural desire to revisit our native land, after so long an absence. In fact, I know no part of Her Majesty's dominions where the soldier is better off as regards mere physical comforts, and it would be ungrateful not to acknowledge the care and attention bestowed upon his health. This admission however in no way affects what I have been endeavouring to urge in these pages, that there is room for extensive reforms and improvements in our military service both at home and abroad; and I think I have demonstrated that attempts to repress by direct and penal restrictions vices that tend to affect the bodily health will, in most cases, fail, unless they are accompanied by measures calculated to elevate the moral condition as well.

It is not to be wondered at, that of all our military stations, India should be preferred by the lower classes of the army. The duty is not severe, and the luxuries as well as the necessaries of life are within the reach of the humblest purse. Here are no manorial or river rights, the invasion of whose privileges is attended with fine or imprisonment. The soldier may range over hill and dale, through savannah and jungle, waging war against all created things, without being called on to render an account of his actions, at least during the term to which his leave extends. When he returns, fatigued after his day's sport, he may sit down and regale himself off fish and game, such as is not often to be found on the tables of the great.

Owing to these advantages there was formerly a great unwillingness on the part of the soldiery to exchange the Indian for the home service; and, when a regiment was recalled, it was usual for numbers to volunteer into that which succeeded it. The habit has diminished within the last few years, but this is entirely attributable to the regulation issued from the Horse Guards in 1836, that instead of a shilling a day pension, for twenty four years' service, the soldier shall only receive sixpence, for the extended period of twenty eight.

It is true that the latter regulation has this condition annexed to it, that every soldier who may have obtained four good conduct stripes at the period of his discharge, shall be entitled to an additional fourpence a day: but when it is recollected how stringent are the rules of the service, and how various the accidents of a military life, the best conducted man may reasonably despair of being placed within this favoured category.

Leaving aside all considerations of humanity, and viewing it as it was intended, simply as an economic measure, it will not be difficult to show that the arrangement is far from being an advantageous one to the country. On being replaced by the 14th Dragoons, out of three hundred men who had joined us from England, within the previous two years, not ten could be found to volunteer into that or any other of the cavalry regiments in India, although the bounty was as high as £3 10.

Being curious to ascertain the cause of a fact so opposed to all former experience, I questioned several, and the uniform answer I received was, that after a twenty-eight years' service in India, a man would be good for nothing in his own country, and that sixpence a day was too miserable a pittance to look forward to as a dependence when his strength for work had failed him.

The consequence was, that the majority of those newly arrived soldiers returned to England, and owing to the regulation as regards height, not being so strict for the Indian as for the home service, they were discharged almost to a man, as being under the proper standard.

The country had, therefore, to pay the expenses of their passage out and home, as well as of their clothing and sustenance, during their training at the cavalry depot, for a period of service little exceeding the time employed in the probation and voyage.

Comment on these facts would be superfluous.

And now, gentle reader, I must bid you farewell. If in these light and unpretending sketches I have at all contributed to your amusement, or if I have thrown out suggestions that may be considered useful or practical in their bearing on the welfare of a class which has but few organs, though many grievances, I shall be amply compensated for the risk that I run of being hunted down by the critics.

Should they weigh me in the balance of literary merit and find me wanting, I must only appeal to your indulgence, and ask you to throw the shelter of your protecting wing over one who, though he has grown old in your service in one capacity, is as yet unfledged and timid in the other.

ALSO FROM LEONAUR
AVAILABLE IN SOFTCOVER OR HARDCOVER WITH DUST JACKET

JOURNALS OF ROBERT ROGERS OF THE RANGERS *by Robert Rogers*—The exploits of Rogers & the Rangers in his own words during 1755-1761 in the French & Indian War.

GALLOPING GUNS *by James Young*—The Experiences of an Officer of the Bengal Horse Artillery During the Second Maratha War 1804-1805.

GORDON *by Demetrius Charles Boulger*—The Career of Gordon of Khartoum.

THE BATTLE OF NEW ORLEANS *by Zachary F. Smith*—The final major engagement of the War of 1812.

THE TWO WARS OF MRS DUBERLY *by Frances Isabella Duberly*—An Intrepid Victorian Lady's Experience of the Crimea and Indian Mutiny.

WITH THE GUARDS' BRIGADE DURING THE BOER WAR *by Edward P. Lowry*—On Campaign from Bloemfontein to Koomati Poort and Back.

THE REBELLIOUS DUCHESS *by Paul F. S. Dermoncourt*—The Adventures of the Duchess of Berri and Her Attempt to Overthrow French Monarchy.

MEN OF THE MUTINY *by John Tulloch Nash & Henry Metcalfe*—Two Accounts of the Great Indian Mutiny of 1857: Fighting with the Bengal Yeomanry Cavalry & Private Metcalfe at Lucknow.

CAMPAIGN IN THE CRIMEA *by George Shuldham Peard*—The Recollections of an Officer of the 20th Regiment of Foot.

WITHIN SEBASTOPOL *by K. Hodasevich*—A Narrative of the Campaign in the Crimea, and of the Events of the Siege.

WITH THE CAVALRY TO AFGHANISTAN *by William Taylor*—The Experiences of a Trooper of H. M. 4th Light Dragoons During the First Afghan War.

THE CAWNPORE MAN *by Mowbray Thompson*—A First Hand Account of the Siege and Massacre During the Indian Mutiny By One of Four Survivors.

BRIGADE COMMANDER: AFGHANISTAN *by Henry Brooke*—The Journal of the Commander of the 2nd Infantry Brigade, Kandahar Field Force During the Second Afghan War.

BANCROFT OF THE BENGAL HORSE ARTILLERY *by N. W. Bancroft*—An Account of the First Sikh War 1845-1846.

AVAILABLE ONLINE AT **www.leonaur.com**
AND FROM ALL GOOD BOOK STORES